DK EYEWITNESS TOP 10 TRAVEL GUIDES

THE ALGARVE

PAUL BERNHARDT

DORLING KINDERSLEY
LONDON • NEW YORK • MUNICH
MELBOURNE • DELHI
WWW.DK.COM

Left **Tiles, Faro** Right **Roman bridge, Tavira**

A Dorling Kindersley Book

www.dk.com

Produced by Blue Island Publishing
Reproduced by Colourscan, Singapore
Printed and bound in Italy by Graphicom

First published in Great Britain in 2003
by Dorling Kindersley Limited
80 Strand, London WC2R 0RL
A Penguin Company

A CIP catalogue record is available from the British Library.

ISBN 0 7513 4843 0

Within each Top 10 list in this book, no hierarchy of quality or popularity is implied. All 10 are, in the editor's opinion, of roughly equal merit.

Contents

The Algarve's Top 10

The information in this DK Eyewitness Top 10 Travel Guide is checked regularly.

Every effort has been made to ensure that this book is as up-to-date as possible at the time of going to press. Some details, however, such as telephone numbers, opening hours, prices, gallery hanging arrangements and travel information are liable to change. The publishers cannot accept responsibility for any consequences arising from the use of this book, nor for any material on third party websites, and cannot guarantee that any website address in this book will be a suitable source of travel information. We value the views and suggestions of our readers very highly. Please write to: Publisher, DK Eyewitness Travel Guides, Dorling Kindersley, 80 Strand, London WC2R 0RL.

Left **Market, Albufeira** Right **Café with castle in the background, Alcoutim**

Around the Algarve

Streetsmart

Left **Sagres harbour** Right **Ponta de Piedade, Lagos**

Key to abbreviations
Adm *admission charge payable* **Free** *no admission charge*

THE ALGARVE'S TOP 10

THE ALGARVE'S TOP 10

TOP 10 Highlights of the Algarve

Folk dancers

The Moors called their al-Gharb the Sunset Land, and visitors have been waxing lyrical ever since. Blessed with a mild winter climate and a sunny disposition, Portugal's playground province remains one of the most popular year-round holiday destinations in southern Europe. Lively coastal resorts spill over ribbons of golden sand in sharp contrast to the quiet villages of the hinterland, where history and tradition go hand in hand.

1 Faro

The biggest city in southern Portugal, Faro is the capital of the Algarve and an important centre of tourism, trade and commerce. Its historic quarter overlooks a pretty marina and the Ria Formosa *(see pp8–11)*.

2 Tavira

Nearly 40 churches endow this elegant riverside town with a romantic and disarmingly timeless air. The Gilão river glides effortlessly through the centre – a Roman bridge connects the two sides of one of the prettiest towns in the Algarve *(see pp12–13)*.

4 Monchique

The Serra da Monchique rises 458 m (1,500 ft), enveloping the hillside town of Monchique and its neighbouring spa centre *(see pp16–17)*.

3 Silves

Once the grandiose capital of the Moorish province of al-Gharb, Silves today is dominated by the ochre ramparts of its huge castle. Lush orange groves blanket the countryside *(see pp14–15)*.

Previous pages **Igreja do Camo, Faro**

Lagos 6

A young, vibrant and carefree spirit imbues this resort. The nearby beaches, pocked with outcrops of sandstone rock, are spectacular *(see pp20–23)*.

5 Loulé

Loulé hosts a colourful weekly market and is a thriving centre for local handicrafts. It is also the gateway to the central hinterland and the Caldeirão mountain range *(see pp18–19)*.

7 Parque Natural da Ria Formosa

One of the most important wetland zones in Europe, the park's expansive lagoon, sand dunes and marshland are a sanctuary for a wealth of wildlife *(see pp24–7)*.

Sagres 8

The supposed location of Henry the Navigator's lauded school of navigation, Sagres sits on an isolated promontory pounded by the Atlantic. Dramatic views along the coast include the Cabo de São Vicente *(see pp28–9)*.

9 Albufeira

This top holiday spot is the Algarve's largest resort, boasting some of the most effervescent nightlife in Portugal. Generous beaches flank bustling esplanades brimming with cafés and trendy clubs *(see pp30–31)*.

10 Vila Real and Castro Marim

These two frontier towns are in earshot of each other but have little in common. Sedate Castro Marim glories in its twin castles. Vila Real de Santo António enjoys a livelier culture *(see pp32–33)*.

TOP 10 Faro Old Town

Faro's venerable Cidade Velha (Old Town) is the city's most interesting quarter and can be appreciated at a leisurely pace on foot. Set within a circle of medieval walls, the whole vicinity is a veritable time capsule reflecting Faro's brief "golden age" in the 16th century. The landmark cathedral and cloistered convent are set alongside a patchwork of narrow, cobbled streets with some inviting cafés and shops. (For Faro's New Town see pp10–11.)

Igreja de Sao Francisco

Free guided tours around Faro's historical centre are conducted daily. Contact the Museu Municipal on (289) 897 400.

Keep an eye out for storks circling with nonchalant abandon in the sky above Faro.

The bar-restaurante Aqui D'El Rei, on Rua do Repouso, is well situated next to the little chapel of Nossa Senhora do Repouso. Another atmospheric place is Restaurante Mesa dos Mouros in front of the cathedral.

Map K6 and town map at back of book • Tourist office by harbour (289) 803 604 • Museu Arqueológico open 10am–6pm Tue & Fri, 2.30–6pm Mon, Wed, Thu & Sat

Top 10 Sights

1. Sé (Cathedral)
2. Museu Arqueológico
3. Igreja de São Francisco
4. Paço Episcopal
5. Arco da Vila
6. Nossa Senhora do Pé da Cruz
7. Nossa Senhora do Repouso
8. Galeria de Arte Arco
9. Galeria de Arte Trem
10. Walls and Towers

1 Sé (Cathedral)

The interior of the 13th-century cathedral *(right)* reveals a fusion of the Gothic, Renaissance and the Baroque: the Capela de Nossa Senhora dos Prazeres, especially, is a jewel of Baroque art, with splendid gilded and lacquered woodcarvings, inlaid marble and a surround of polished *azulejos*.

2 Museu Arqueológico

Gargoyles in the shape of animals embellish the delightfully secluded Renaissance cloisters of this former convent which imaginatively incorporates the museum. Highlights include a huge Roman floor mosaic, a collection of Moorish oil lamps and an exquisite 16th-century eucharistic safe. *(See p44)*

3 Igreja de São Francisco

Stunning *azulejos* panels depicting the life of St Francis adorn the walls of this 17th-century church. The vault contains an outstanding polychrome panel showing the coronation of the Virgin.

4 Paço Episcopal

The original building was plundered and damaged by the Earl of Essex in 1596. Rebuilt again after the 1755 earthquake, it's still in use today, but closed to the public.

5 Arco da Vila

The grandiose arch *(left)* was inaugurated in 1812. Tucked inside the arch is an 11th-century horseshoe gate, which is believed to have been built by the Moors and is the only one of its kind in the Algarve.

6 Nossa Senhora do Pé da Cruz

Overlooking a pretty square, this 17th-century chapel is home to a lovely configuration of gilded wood carvings and a series of whimsical oil panels depicting scenes from the Old Testament. At the rear is a chapel with an 18th-century *azulejos* crucifix *(right)*.

8 Galeria de Arte Arco

Perched on top of the city walls, the Arco art gallery is worth a visit if only for its superb view of the Ria Formosa. Art buffs will also appreciate the exhibitions which reflect the very best in contemporary Portuguese art.

7 Nossa Senhora do Repouso

Set into a niche in the castle walls, this small chapel lies in the shadow of the medieval Gate of Rest. Popular legend has it that Afonso III, fresh from his victory over the Moors, rested here.

9 Galeria de Arte Trem

Housed off the main square and part of a former military barracks, the Trem art gallery shares floorspace with an excavated Roman arch built on Moorish foundations. The venue is a favourite among modern artists, both home-grown and visiting from abroad.

10 Walls and Towers

The original castle walls were Roman, vestiges of which can still be seen today. The rest of the fortifications are the result of 16th-century labour *(right)*. The exception is the Byzantine towers, added soon after the collapse of the Roman Empire and incongruous in their pentagonal design.

The Story of Faro

The Phoenicians and Carthaginians established trading posts on the banks of the Ria Formosa, which flourished into a major Roman port known as Ossonoba. The Moors fortified the town but couldn't halt the armies of Afonso III, who captured the city in 1249. A period of prosperity ended in 1596 when the Earl of Essex plundered and burned the city. Rebuilding began, but the 1755 earthquake destroyed it again, forever altering the urban makeup.

Left **Faro marina** Centre **Ermida de Santo António do Alte** Right **Tiles on the outer city walls**

TOP 10 Faro New Town and Riverfront

Igreja do Carmo

1 Igreja do Carmo/ Capela dos Ossos

A feast of Baroque decoration, gilded with the finest Brazilian gold leaf. A macabre offering, though, is the Capela dos Ossos (Chapel of Bones), which is lined with the skulls and bones of more than a thousand monks. *Largo do Carmo • Closed Sun • Adm*

2 Museu Marítimo

An engaging cruise around the Algarve's maritime heritage, from the Golden Age of Discoveries to the intricacies of catching tuna in the present day. *(See p45)*

3 Teatro de Lethes

Once a Jesuit college, this little Italianate gem dates from 1874 and is a beautiful example of a late 19th-century provincial playhouse. Now sparkling after extensive restoration, the venue hosts occasional plays, concerts and recitals. *Rua de Portugal 58 • 289 820 300*

Teatro de Lethes

4 Science Alive Centre

An engrossing and highly original interactive study centre promoting scientific and technological awareness. The centre invites you to climb up to the "observatory" for a voyage into the Milky Way. *Rua Com. Francisco Manuel • Closed Mon • Adm*

5 Museu Etnógrafico

Find out what rural Algarve looked like bereft of modern conveniences in this nostalgic display of sepia photographs, early 20th-century looms, faded ceramics, kitchenware and dainty embroidered aprons. *Praça da Liberdade • 9am–12:30pm, 2–5:30pm Mon–Fri*

6 Cemitério dos Judeus

To the northeast, the city's 19th-century cemetery is laid out in the traditional Sephardic way with children buried near the entrance, women in the centre and men at the back. The Jewish community no longer exists in Faro. *9:30–12:30 Mon–Fri*

7 Ermida de Santo António do Alte

Built in 1355, this is one of the oldest buildings in Faro. A hop up the steps at the side of the chapel is rewarded with a fine city panorama. *Rua da Merlim*

8 Café Aliança

The charming, early 20th-century tea house doubles up as a photographic gallery with framed images of a bygone Faro. *Rua Dr F. Gomes*

9 Ilha de Faro

A natural link in a chain of sand dune islands that constitute part of the Parque Natural da Ria Formosa *(see pp24–7)*, this is very popular in summer but near-deserted off-season. *Map K6*

Parasailing, Ilha de Faro

10 Palácio dos Bívar

This late 18th-century former private residence is generally regarded as the finest example of Neoclassical architecture in the Algarve. *Rua Conselheiro Bivar*

Faro's Top 10 Personalities

1. **Mohammed ben Said ben Hárun** Gave Faro its name in 11th century.
2. **Afonso III** Captured city in 1249.
3. **Samuel Gacon** Produced first printed manuscript in Portugal (1487).
4. **Queen Catarina** Completed Convento de Nossa Senhora da Assunção.
5. **2nd Earl of Essex** Sacked Faro in 1596.
6. **Bishop Francisco Gomes** (1739–1816) Rebuilt city after quake.
7. **Francisco Xavier Fabri** (1761–1817) Architect.
8. **Manuel Bívar** (1861–1901) Prominent member of illustrious family.
9. **Dr Amadeu Ferreira de Almeida Carvalho** (1876–1966) Gave art collection to museum.
10. **Carlos Porfírio** (1895–1970) One of Portugal's greatest modern artists.

Cosmopolitan Faro

Statue of Bishop Francisco Gomes

Faro's history (see p9) *and cosmopolitan flavour continues beyond the obvious Moorish and Christian features of the old town. New town houses sprang up outside the city walls in the 17th and 18th centuries, Mannerist in style. Battlements built during the War of Restoration (1640–68) enclosed this new urban area. Modernday Faro capitalizes on a vibrant social life and rich artistic heritage. Alluring historical buildings can be found alongside modern museums and quaint pavement cafés. The city boasts a colourful agenda of music, song and dance. As exciting, in fact, as the city's restaurants, where the best traditional cuisine of the Algarve can be sampled.*

Light and airy café in Faro

Top 10 Tavira

With its timeless atmosphere, traditional character and dignified charm, it's small wonder that many consider the elegant riverside town of Tavira to be the most pleasant and picturesque in the Algarve. Sited on both sides of the Rio Gilão, the town is perhaps best known for its abundance of churches – nearly 40 in all, with some dating back to the 13th century. The history of Tavira itself, though, is much older. Tavira's prosperity today relies to a great degree on tourism, although not to the detriment of the town's peaceful ambience.

3 Castle Remains

Crowning a cobble-stoned knoll, the surviving walls of this Moorish fort envelope a spruce garden. The view from the ramparts takes in the town's outline of pyramid-shaped rooftops to distant Ilha de Tavira. *(See p52)*

Fishing boat

Guided walking tours depart from the tourism office at 10am and 3pm Mon–Fri. Call (281) 321 946.

Quatro Águas is lovely at sunset, but beware of mosquitoes near the river.

There are two cafés in Praça da Republica, near the Roman bridge. Charming Café Veneza has a pavement terrace and serves lovely fig cakes. Next door, the busy Romana serves light meals.

- *Map M4 and town map at back of book*
- *Tourist information Rua da Galeria 9*
- *(281) 322 511*

Top 10 Sights

1. Igreja da Misericórdia
2. Igreja de Santa Maria do Castelo
3. Castle Remains
4. Igreja do São Paulo
5. Ponta Romana
6. Capela da Nossa Senhora da Consolação
7. Quatro Águas
8. Ilha de Tavira
9. Fortaleza do Rato
10. Arabic-Style Lattice Doors

1 Igreja da Misericórdia

Townsfolk are justly proud that this 16th-century church is considered the Algarve's most important Renaissance monument. Its striking arched portal is surmounted by statues of saints.

2 Igreja de Santa Maria do Castelo

The clock face of this church is a familiar landmark *(below)*. Inside are the tombs of the Moors' nemesis Dom Paio Peres Correia and seven of his Christian knights.

Roman bridge (Ponta Romana)

4 Igreja do São Paulo

Facing a colourful and well-tended public garden, this 17th-century church – originally part of a monastery – has a transept paved with small lozenge-shaped bricks. These were fashioned in Seville, Spain, and decorated with delicate flower motifs – a unique design in Portugal.

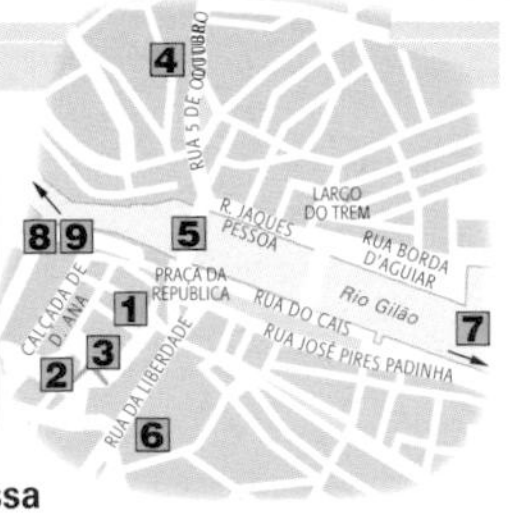

5 Ponta Romana

The foundations of the low, arched stone bridge spanning the Rio Gilão are Roman in origin. Illuminated at night in a romantic ethereal glow, the bridge is a favourite subject for artists.

6 Capela da Nossa Senhora da Consolação

A little gem of a chapel, heaving with polychrome tiles dating from the 17th century. The simple retable is illuminated with a series of paintings.

7 Quatro Águas

This beauty spot southeast of Tavira overlooks a sleepy lagoon and boasts some fine seafood restaurants. It is the jumping-off point for Ilha de Tavira. Quatro Águas is the name of the local style of rooftops.

8 Ilha de Tavira

A regular ferry service makes for an easy escape to the marvellous sand dune island, a popular resort during the summer months for its excellent swimming. It lies within the boundaries of the Ria Formosa nature park *(see pp24–7)*.

9 Fortaleza do Rato

The elements have not been kind to the modest ruins of the "rat's fort", which was built at the mouth of the Gilão river in the 16th century. Its lichen-encrusted walls do, however, afford a broad and uplifting salt-braced vista across the lagoon and Ilha de Tavira.

10 Arabic-Style Lattice Doors

Built into the façades of some of Tavira's back street properties are delightful examples of *portas de reixa* (lattice panelled doors; *right)*. Arabic in design, each panel is made of finely interwoven lengths of wood. They evoke the Moorish influence still inherent in the region.

Local Cuisine

Tavira's seafood specialities include *acorda marisco*, a concoction of cockles, prawns and clams sunk in a thick bread-based soup, and *lulas cheias*, which is tender squid filled with cured meats and rice, and braised in an onion and tomato sauce. Santa Luzia, a village southwest of Tavira, is justly regarded the octopus capital of the Algarve. Order the octopus rice stew *(arroz de polvo)*.

Top 10 Silves

Known as Xelb in Arabic, the 30,000-strong Moorish settlement prospered until 1189 when Dom Sancho I laid siege to it with the help of an English crusader army. The Christians finally gained total control in 1242. These days, Silves is better known as a centre of citrus fruit and cork production. The castle, with its sandstone walls casting a sepia wash over the town below, is a stark reminder of Silves' once-powerful past.

Cathedral door

A pair of binoculars come in handy when scanning the countryside from the castle.

The Café Inglês just below the castle is open daily for wholesome homemade fare. A wonderful rooftop terrace is open in summer.

Café Rosa, just off Rua 25 Abril, fronts a peaceful square and is decorated inside with lovely *azulejos* panels. A perfect place for a coffee.

Map F4 and town plan at back of book • Tourist information Rua 25 de Abril 26–28, tel (282) 442 255 • Museu Arqueológico open 10am–6pm Tue–Sun • Museu de Cortiça open 9.30–12.45 & 2pm–9.45pm (6pm winter) daily

Top 10 Sights

1. Castelo
2. Museu Arqueológico
3. Sé (Cathedral)
4. Fábrica do Inglês Show Ground
5. Museu da Cortiça
6. Cruz de Portugal
7. Parque Biológico
8. Igreja da Misericórdia
9. Ponta Romana
10. Ancient Pillory

1 Castelo

The grandest monument to Islamic rule in the Algarve, Silves Castle is a stronghold of dynamic proportions, built on the site of 4th-century Roman fortifications. Views from the ramparts are superb.

2 Museu Arqueológico

An engrossing museum which superbly charts human existence in the region over the course of 8,000 years, from the Palaeolithic period to the mid-16th century. *(See p44)*

3 Sé (Cathedral)

Dating from the 13th century, the town's Gothic cathedral was the seat of the Algarve see until 1580, when that honour was transferred to the bishops' palace in Faro. There are a number of curiosities to catch the eye, including petulant-looking gargoyles on the apse, and Crusader tombs.

4 Fábrica do Inglês Show Ground

A permanent show ground with a host of lively bars and restaurants and the Museu da Cortiça. In the summer months the venue sways to daily concerts and dance performances. Evenings are brought to an end with the spectacular "Aquavision" laser show.

5 Museu da Cortiça

Winner of the Best Industrial Museum in Europe, this extraordinary exhibition, housed in a former cork factory, chronicles the harvesting techniques and the methods used to process and manufacture cork *(below, also see p45)*.

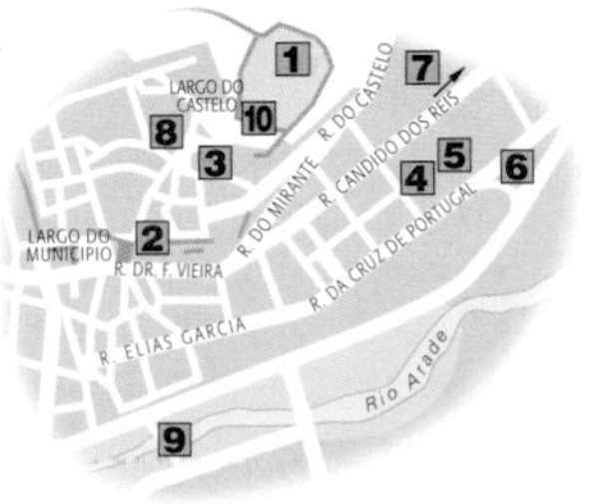

6 Cruz de Portugal

Standing rather incongruously next to a main road, the exquisite 16th-century granite cross *(above)* is said to have been a gift to the city from Dom Manuel I.

7 Parque Biológico

Deer, wild boar, pheasants, grouse, falcons and even a family of baboons are some of the permanent residents of the secluded game park, 8 km (4 miles) northeast of Silves.

8 Igreja da Misericórdia

The highly decorative side doorway above ground level possibly served as the original entrance and shows the influence of the 16th-century "Manueline" style. The main chapel has a ribbed vault and Renaissance altarpiece.

9 Ponta Romana

Only the foundations of this pretty whitewashed bridge date back to Roman times. The rest of the structure is medieval in origin. These days it's closed to traffic, but not long ago the bridge was the only access point across the River Arade.

10 Ancient Pillory

A common symbol of municipal power across Portugal, the pillory standing near the castle was rebuilt from 16th-century remains. Topped by a decorative crown with four sinewy wrought-iron dragons jutting out from the stem, it is the only such example of its kind in the Algarve.

Moorish Silves

As Xelb, Silves was the capital of the Moorish province of Al-Gharb and by 1053 was a crowded metropolis. Writers, poets, scientists, lawmakers and philosophers lived here, and the shadows of several minarets fell across docks, a shipyard, public baths, a synagogue and church. By the mid-12th century, however, Silves started to decline. Nonetheless, the legacy of 500 years of Moorish rule can still be seen in the local architecture, fields of orange, almond, fig and carob trees, and in the Portuguese language itself.

Top 10 Monchique

This spruce and engaging little market town nestles in the Serra da Monchique, a densely wooded canvas of eucalyptus, chestnut, pine and cork trees interrupted by tracts of barren moorland. A welcome change from beaches and villas, Monchique is all about cobbled streets and rural sentiment. The local medronho *– firewater distilled from the berries of the arbutus (strawberry tree) – is the finest available anywhere.*

Monchique town centre

Monchique resident António Maria Valéiro organizes tours to *medronho* distilleries – (282) 912 710.

Monchique is also known for its small wooden "scissor" chairs, which neatly fold up between use and make good gifts.

Reasonably priced cafés and restaurants cluster round the central bus station.

Down in Caldas de Monchique, Café-Restaurante 1692 has a marvellous terrace that spills out onto the square.

Map E3 • Tourist info office Largo de Chorões • (282) 911 189

Top 10 Sights

1. Igreja Matriz
2. Nossa Senhora do Desterro
3. Restaurante Central
4. Caldas de Monchique
5. Termas de Monchique
6. Fóia
7. Serra de Monchique Bio-Park
8. Igreja de São Sebastião
9. Picota
10. Barranco de Pisões

1 Igreja Matriz

An intriguing Manueline doorway *(above)* greets visitors to Monchique's 16th-century parish church. The twisted columns resemble lengths of gnarled rope. Inside, the capitals of the columns in the three naves are similarly fashioned, suggesting a nautical theme.

2 Nossa Senhora do Desterro

A mysterious air pervades the ruins of the Franciscan monastery. Severely damaged by the 1755 earthquake, its empty shell echoes to cooing doves and the rustle of leaves from an immense magnolia – possibly the biggest in Europe – which rears out of the old garden.

View from the Peak of Fóia in the Serra da Monchique

3 Restaurante Central

It's worth visiting the restaurant *(below)*, if only to relish the sight of thousands of business cards and doodles left by satisfied customers from around the world. At least take a glimpse through the window.

5 Termas de Monchique

The delightful thermal spa complex is set under a lush canopy of pine and eucalyptus. Though modern, it retains a pleasant, bygone air.

4 Caldas de Monchique

The Romans were bowled over by this cosy hamlet in the Monchique hills and totally enamoured by the hot, curative properties of its waters *(above)*.

6 Fóia

For the most stunning landscape views in the entire Algarve, head for the peak of Fóia. At 902 m (2,959 ft), this is the highest point in the Serra de Monchique.

7 Serra de Monchique Bio-Park

Nearly 1,000 km (500 miles) of mapped and sign-posted footpath, cycle track and bridleway snakes its way through the Monchique hills. It is a haven for wildlife, including the rare and elusive Iberian lynx.

8 Igreja de São Sebastião

The church *(right)* contains a beautifully sculptured 17th-century figure of Nossa Senhora de Desterro.

9 Picota

At 773 m (2,536 ft), this second peak doesn't quite command the same all-round vista as Fóia, but Picota is steeper and pleasantly wooded. Its location affords beautiful views that take in long sweeps of scented meadows and a sparkling, distant sea.

10 Barranco de Pisões

A captivating little beauty spot about 4 km (2 miles) north of Monchique, the hideaway is known locally for its ancient waterwheel and 1,000-year-old plane tree.

Monchique's Spa

According to legend, if you take a sip from the fountain of love, an ancient font hiding in the dappled woods behind Caldas de Monchique, you'll fall in love with life. The waters are said to be good for a whole host of maladies including rheumatic and digestive disorders and skin complaints. The Romans certainly thought so, as did Dom João II. Today's visitors are offered a range of water-based therapy, using vapours, water jets, hydromassage, steam and hot algae.

TOP 10 Loulé

The pleasant inland town of Loulé is renowned for its traditional handicrafts and splendid market. The Romans first settled on the spot now occupied by the castle, but it was the Moors for whom Loulé was to become a conurbation of some importance. Remnants of their presence are still manifest in the belltower of Igreja São Clemente, formally a minaret. The castle is also Moorish in origin. Almonds and figs have been essential to the local economy for centuries.

Largo de Cargo, Roundabout

A wide and inventive array of wickerwork can be purchased at Manuel Caliço Grosso, on the corner of Rua João de Deus and Rua Serpa Pinto.

One of the best places to eat is Pastelaria Baguetomania, just off Avenida 25 Abril. Based on a Brazilian concept, you only pay as much as your plate weighs. Open 7am–2pm daily.

For a more traditional setting, order a *bica* (small coffee) at Café Calcinha, Praça da República, 67.

Map J4 • Market Praça da República 7am–2pm Saturday • Loulé Carnival in Feb (Shrove Tuesday)

Top 10 Sights

1. Castelo
2. Museu Municipal
3. Igreja Matriz de São Lourenço
4. Capela Nossa Senhora da Conceição
5. Market
6. Museu dos Frutos Secos
7. Igreja São Clemente
8. Rua da Barbaca
9. Igreja da Misericórdia
10. Loulé Carnival

1 Castelo

The ruins underwent restoration during the 19th century and today house a museum (below) and tourism office. Visitors are rewarded with grand views of the town from its battlements *(see p52)*.

2 Museu Municipal

The best attraction of the museum *(right)* is the first-floor recreation of a traditional Algarve kitchen with its 19th-century utensils and tableware. There are also Bronze Age ceramics. *(See p45)*

4 Capela Nossa Senhora da Conceição

The subdued ambience of the quaint 17th-century chapel is lifted by *azulejos* and a Baroque altarpiece. The ceiling panel was by Loulé painter Rasquinho.

Loulé Market

3 Igreja Matriz de São Lourenço

About 8 km (5 miles) south-east of Loulé, at Almansil, Blue and white *azulejo* panels grace the walls of the chancel, nave and magnificent trompe-l'oeil cupola of this decorative church.

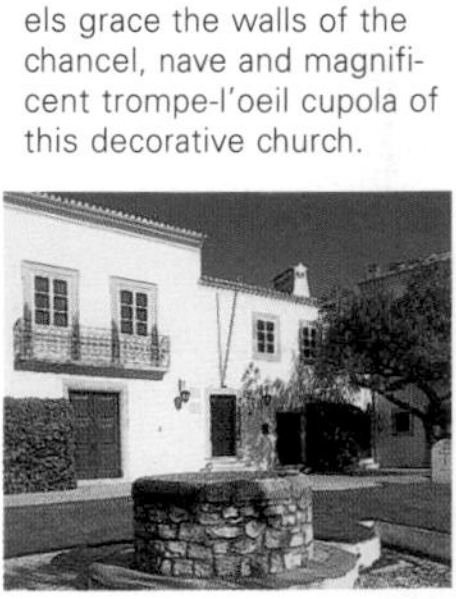

5 Market

Mixed herbs, cheeses *(right)* and red chilli peppers vie for the eye with sweet figs, marzipan cakes and golden honey. Elsewhere, kaleidoscopes of flowers, the freshest of fish, the ripest of fruit and a variety of genuine handicrafts make a visit here an unforgettable shopping experience.

6 Museu dos Frutos Secos

The highly original museum focuses on early harvesting methods for figs, carob and almond fruit. Built in homage to a local businessman.

7 Igreja São Clemente

Loulé's Muslim faithful were once summoned to prayer from the balcony of the lofty belltower which originally served as a minaret. The *azulejo*-clad Capela de Nossa Senhora da Consolação and the Capela de São Brás's Baroque altarpiece are Christian highlights.

8 Rua da Barbaca

Running parallel to the castle walls, Rua da Barbaca is home to many of Loulé's craftsmen *(left)* who busy away the day, fashioning items in copper and brass, leather and wood. Superbly finished saddles and the ubiquitous *cataplana* cooking vessel are some of the items for sale.

9 Igreja da Misericórdia

The entrance has typical Manueline embellishments, such as heavily carved rope rounded off with twisted pinnacles. Opposite stands a cross from the same period.

10 Loulé Carnival

The biggest, brightest and rowdiest of the Algarve's Carnival celebrations *(see p58)*. Costume-clad revellers shake, rattle and roll to hybrid Latin rhythm and African-style percussion.

Traditional Crafts

It was the inauguration of an artisans' fair back in 1291 that forged Loulé's reputation as a manufacturing centre. Many of the techniques used 800 years ago are still employed today. Ceramics are popular with tourists. In many local villages, women still pleat the leaves of dwarf palms to make hats, baskets and rugs; jute fibre is used to stitch pretty rag dolls. Saddleries tucked away in quiet hamlets supply harnesses for mules, and old wooden looms are used to produce shawls and blankets.

Lagos

Lively, colourful and cheerful, Lagos is probably the most popular resort in the Algarve. Its easy-going atmosphere nourishes a predominantly young crowd who are attracted to the resort's bargain-stacked shops, welter of bars and restaurants, some of the hippest nightlife on the south coast and, of course, close proximity to lovely beaches and cliffs. Punctuating this cosmopolitan hubris is a rich historical vein, a source of great pride to the local population.

2 Fortaleza da Ponta da Bandeira

Accessible via drawbridge, this squat, tidy 17th-century fortress was built to defend the harbour. Nowadays, its sturdy ramparts protect a small museum dedicated to the Age of Discoveries.

Cafés in the town centre

For a boat trip to the grottoes, embark from Avenida dos Desrobimentos, in front of the marina. This way you'll pass the beautiful Dona Ana beach.

The open-air café next to Praça Infante Dom Henrique is an ideal spot for an afternoon coffee under the shade of swaying palm.

For sweet almond delicacies and Italian ice-cream, call in at Taquelim Gonçalves on the marina.

Map D5 • Museu Regional, Rua General Alberto Silveira • 9:30am–12:30pm, 2pm–5pm Tue–Sun • Adm €1.95 • (282) 762 301 to book guided group tours in winter

Top 10 Sights

1. Igreja de Santo António
2. Fortaleza da Ponte da Bandeira
3. Museu Regional
4. Town Walls
5. Ponta da Piedade
6. Praia de Dona Ana
7. Igreja de Santa Maria
8. Slave Market Site
9. Meia Praia
10. Barragém de Bravura

1 Igreja de Santo António

This 18th-century church *(above)* is a dazzling jewel in the Algarve crown. Inside, the profusion of gilded and painted woodwork positively overflows with ebullience. Everything the Baroque age is famous for is here: double-chinned cherubs, mythical beasts and ripened fruit.

3 Museu Regional

This wonderful and totally absorbing museum houses an extraordinary collection of artifacts and oddities, plus one or two national treasures *(see pp22–3)*. Of particular note are the Roman mosaics, the 1504 town charter, vestments embroidered in gold and a bizarre acquisition of animal freaks, pickled and sealed in rows of glass jars.

For highlights of the Museu Regional **See following pages**

4 Town Walls

The foundations of the walls *(right)* date from Roman times, strengthened during Arab and Christian occupation. Restored in the 16th century, the best preserved section encases a Manueline window from which Dom Sebastião is said to have addressed townsfolk before going to Alcácer-Quibir *(see p23)*.

5 Ponta da Piedade

Parts of the dramatic headland, 3 km (2 miles) northwest of town, resemble a huge wedge of crumbling ginger cake. Standing beneath gnarled sandstone cliffs are towering outcrops of umber-hued rock, hiding a warren of caves and grottoes. A lighthouse crowns the promontory, a suitably romantic location for a sunset finale.

6 Praia de Dona Ana

The photographer's favourite, postcards bearing the image of this beach *(right)* have been mailed around the world. Wedged between cliffs in a small sheltered bay, Dona Ana is often said to resemble an ancient amphitheatre. The stalagmite-shaped cylindrical towers of sandstone rising out of the shallows could pass for Roman columns.

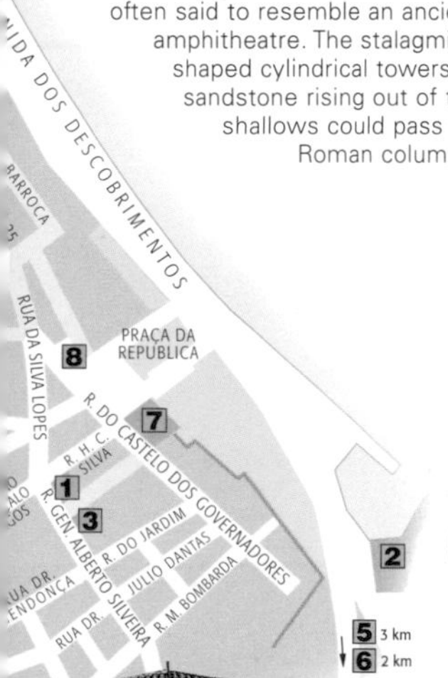

7 Igreja de Santa Maria

The town's parish church dates back to the 16th century, although much of what you see today was rebuilt in the 19th century. The church, however, still retains its Renaissance doorway complete with Doric columns and busts of São Pedro (St Peter) and São Paulo (St Paul) on either side of the archivolt.

8 Slave Market Site

The northeast corner of Praça Infante Dom Henrique *(above)* is site of Europe's first slave market in the 15th century.

9 Meia Praia

Meia Praia translates as "Half Beach", which is curious given that, at 4 km (2.5 miles) long, its huge expanse of sand is one of the longest beaches in the Algarve. But that's good news for those seeking privacy, and for windsurfers and paragliders who take regular advantage of the fresh south-westerlies.

10 Barragém de Bravura

Located 10 km (6 miles) north of Lagos, the immense man-made reservoir tapped by a somewhat incongruous dam is a veritable oasis of peace and tranquillity. A picturesque lake stretches out beneath a broad, rustic backdrop of rolling hills peppered with eucalyptus trees. It is a great place for a picnic.

Left **Altar, Igreja de Santo António** Centre **External entrance to the church** Right **Cork carving**

Highlights of Lagos Museu Regional

1 Igreja de Santo António

Before entering the museum, it is worth taking time to appreciate the adjacent church. The 18th-century interior, with its fantastic excess of gilded Baroque carvings, is sumptuous and quite compelling, and its finery whets the appetite for the museum next door.

São Gonçalo de Lagos

2 Foral Dado a Lagos (Town Charter)

In terms of historical value, this is a priceless exhibit. Conferred on Lagos by Dom Manuel I in 1504, the beautiful leather volume binds a manuscript written on parchment. An exercise in fine calligraphy, the opening page is embossed with gold leaf.

3 Altar de Campanha

An extraordinary 17th-century mobile altar that was carried by Portuguese troops into the field and used for prayer between military engagements. A carved statue of St Anthony rests on top of the altar, which is inlaid with gold leaf.

4 Priest's Vestments

A number of fine examples are displayed in the Sacred Art wing of the museum, but the most outstanding garment is the one worn at the Mass attended by Dom Sebastião in 1578 before his disastrous incursion into Morocco. The robe is hand embroidered with gold.

5 São Gonçalo de Lagos

A delightful anomaly, the 18th-century statue of Lagos' patron saint is incorporated into the door of a cupboard used by the priests of the time to store their shoes and robes. Ask the custodian to open it up.

Artifacts in the entrance to Lagos Museu Regional

6 Manuel Cabanas Room

Manuel Cabanas (1902–95) was Portugal's greatest exponent of wood engraving. This collection, bequeathed by his estate, is a small but select representation of a much

The official museum tour incorporates the adjoining Igreja de Santo António, which is a national monument

Portrait of Estevão Amarante

greater portfolio on display in Vila Real de Santo António *(see p32).*

7 Portrait of Estevão Amarante

The life-size portrait of the late Portuguese thespian Estevão Amarante was painted by Fernando Santos in 1936. As you walk past the image the subsequent change in perspective appears to make Sr Amarante's left foot move with you – an eerie sensation indeed!

8 Senhora do Forte Model Village

Housed in the Ethnographic Hall is a remarkable labour of love: a huge scale model of an imaginary Algarve coastal town. Constructed with breathtaking attention to detail, it took Lagos resident Pedro Reis 5,300 hours to build over a three-year, seven-month period.

9 Cork Altarpiece

A mini masterpiece of cork whittling, this framed, three-dimensional retable was carved by Silves resident Francisco Figueiras in 1907. Brimming with fancy filigree, it's so delicate that it will seem almost to tremble under your very gaze.

10 Opus Vermiculatum Mosaic

The impressive, near-complete Roman mosaic was unearthed in 1933 by the museum's founder, Dr José Formosinho, near Budens, 10 km (6 miles) west of Lagos. Complementing it is a smaller but wholly intact example discovered at Abicada, 2 km (1 mile) east of Portimão.

Story of Lagos

Old entrance to city

Lagos has "welcomed" visitors ever since the Phoenicians and Carthaginians established settlements along the banks of its superb natural harbour well over 2,000 years ago. Under subsequent Roman occupation the town became known as Lacobriga and flourished as a busy port. The ever-cautious Moors built a double ring of ramparts around its centre, but that was not enough to repel the Christians who conquered the city in 1241. During the 15th century – the period of Portugal's Golden Age of Discoveries – Henry the Navigator's caravels departed Lagos shipyards bound for far-flung African climes, and the town quickly became a centre for trade in ivory, gold, silver and other exotic merchandise. A far more unsavoury enterprise was also spawned...slavery! In 1578, Dom Sebastião bade Lagos farewell before heading off to Alcàcer-Quibir, only to perish on the Moroccan battlefield along with 8,000 of his hapless troops. Lagos became the capital of the Algarve in 1576 and remained so until 1756 when the honour was transferred first to Tavira and then finally to Faro. By that time, however, much of the Algarve, Lagos included, lay in ruins after the devastating 1755 earthquake.

The harbour

TOP 10 Parque Natural da Ria Formosa

The Parque Natural da Ria Formosa comprises an extensive lagoon area that follows 60 km (37 miles) of coastline between Manta Rota and Vale do Lobo. Made up of sand dune islands, marshland, saltpans and shimmering freshwater lakes, the habitat is sanctuary for an astonishing assortment of flora and fauna, including birds such as the rare purple gallinule. The park headquarters at Quinta de Marim, 3 km (1.5 miles) east of Olhão, has a first-class visitor centre.

San Lorenzo (see p46)

Wear a pair of stout walking boots if you are planning to follow the nature trails, and put on warm clothing in winter.

Photographers in the hides will need a telephoto lens of at least 300 mm.

There is a weekday restaurant-bar in the Quinta de Marim Visitor Centre, and special picnic zones within the park.

Map K–L6 • Quinta de Marim • (289) 704 134 for info regarding accommodation and conservation projects • 9am–12.30pm, 2pm–5.30pm daily • €1.5

Top 10 Sights

1. São Lourenço Nature Trail
2. Quinta do Lago Nature Trail
3. Portuguese Water Dog Kennels
4. Freshwater Lagoons and Hides
5. Coastal Conifer Woods
6. Recuperation Centre for Birds
7. Tide Mill
8. Roman Salting Tanks
9. Coastal Dunes
10. João Lucio's House

1 São Lourenço Nature Trail

One of the most rewarding introductions to the reserve is to follow the 3.2 km (1.8 mile) São Lourenço nature trail *(below)*. It will bring you into close contact with two different types of wetland: the salt marshes and the freshwater lagoons.

2 Quinta do Lago Nature Trail

A partly shady trail *(above)* which highlights the flora of two widely differing ecosystems: woodland and marsh. The path wends past umbrella and maritime pines.

Coastal dunes

3 Portuguese Water Dog Kennels

These busy kennels allow visitors to see and learn about the unique, web-footed Portuguese water dog *(see p26)*. The dog was bred back from near-extinction here.

4 Freshwater Lagoons and Hides

The freshwater lagoons provide vital refuge for nesting and migrating birds, and harbour a miscellany of aquatic mammals. The view from the observation hides *(right)* brings this sparkling marine oasis into sharp focus.

5 Coastal Conifer Woods

Coastal conifer woodland is sparse in the eastern Algarve, but where it occurs it provides an efficient means of coastal protection and adds to the diverse beauty of the terrain.

6 Recuperation Centre for Birds

This innovative hospital for sick and injured birds has an area for visitors to observe the recuperating "patients", which often include birds of prey, via closed-circuit TV.

7 Tide Mill

A late 13th-century invention, tide mills were once very common in the lagoon and river estuaries along the Portuguese coastline. Power was obtained by utilizing the change in water levels associated with shifting tides. The example on the Ria Formosa *(below)* is the last of 30 that used to operate.

8 Roman Salting Tanks

Five Roman salting tanks *(above)* can be explored near the fresh-water lagoons. Dating from the 2nd century AD, they were once used for salting fish prior to their distribution all over Rome's empire.

9 Coastal Dunes

The sweeping tracts of sand guarding the mouth of the estuary constitute a fragile environment, partly held together by the vegetation that has colonized them.

10 João Lucio's House

João Lucio, 19th-century poet, lawyer and former mayor of Olhão, owned much of the land on which Quinta de Marim is now situated. His former villa, near the river's edge, is now an environmental study centre *(below)*.

Left **Purple gallinule** Right **Rugged coastal terrain of the Ria Formosa**

TOP 10 Animals of the Ria Formosa

1 Purple Gallinule

Very rare, this striking bird is reclusive in nature and tends to play hide-and-seek in cattail that sprouts along the edge of the freshwater lagoons. A dark-coloured relative of the moorhen, there are just 20 couples in residence.

Greater flamingo

2 Portuguese Water Dog

Mild-mannered and intelligent by nature, this web-footed canine is unique to Portugal and one of the earliest known breeds in the world. A superb diver, the dog has won long-standing affection with the fishing community and with visitors to the park.

3 Mediterranean Chameleon

This is a treat indeed for anyone lucky enough to spy one of these remarkable creatures, wrapped as it is in a colour-co-ordinated skin. Hibernating from December to March, the best time to see this bulbous-eyed reptile out and about is on early spring mornings.

4 Greater Flamingo

There's no more majestic a sight than a pink band of flamingo panning for food on the salinas. Large flocks of these graceful birds gather in the park during autumn en route to winter breeding grounds, but they can also be spotted in the summer.

5 European Pond Terrapin

A whimsical little member of the chelonian family, this diminutive amphibian is fond of lakes, ponds and calm rivers. It is usually only detected as it darts for shelter through the water at the sound of approaching feet. Tread lightly!

6 Azur-Winged Magpie

A handsome, cheeky bird frequently heard chattering in small groups among the pine-woods near Quinta do Lago. Easily recognized by its sooty crown and nape, the blue flash of its wing feathers makes this species particularly alluring in flight.

7 Hoopoe

An exotic-looking bird with a lovely salmon-pink crest, the hoopoe is the golfer's companion, often seen probing for cutworm on the manicured

Pond terrapin

grass of fairways across the Algarve. Primarily a summer visitor, some individuals remain in the region throughout winter.

8 Fiddler Crab

Often seen scuttling in panic across the mud at low tide, the male of the species has one of its pincers (left or right) considerably more developed than the other. Its European distribution is confined wholly to the Iberian peninsula.

9 Viperine Snake

The Great Pretender, this snake is distinguished by its zig-zag dorsal line and chestnut-

Fiddler crab

coloured scales, which imitate those of a viper. If disturbed it will rear up, inflate its neck and spit. But it's all theatrics – the snake is completely harmless.

10 Little Tern

The little tern's favoured nesting site in Portugal is along the Ria Formosa but the fact that it nests on the sand means that breeding is, at best, precarious.

Top 10 Plants in the Park

Dunes

1. Marram grass (helps support the dune)
2. Sea holly (top of dune)
3. Thrift (centre of dune)
4. Sea daffodil (delicate white flowers in summer)

Coastal Woodland

5. Furze (thorny shrub)

Salt Marsh

6. Cord grass (endures long submersion)
7. Sea lavender (identified by spikes of white, pink or mauve flowers)
8. Sea purslane (lance-shaped leaves and purple flowers)

Freshwater Lagoon

9. Cattail (cylindrical spike)
10. Rush (ideal shelter for aquatic wildlife)

Preserving the Environment

Want to spend more time at Ria Formosa and help preserve it for future generations? The Centro de Educação Ambiental de Marim (Marim Environmental Educational Centre – CEAM) works to protect the environment and promote a balanced and sustainable development of the park's natural resources. It runs a number of conservation projects manned by enthusiastic volunteers, and members of the public are welcome to join in. Call in at the CEAM's offices in Quinta de Marim for more details if you want to be involved in the coastal clean-ups, irrigation work, weeding and pruning and the maintenance of the kennels, aquariums and the veterinary hospital. Volunteers get free accommodation at the centre.

Lagoon, Parque Natural da Ria Formosa

Top 10 Sagres

Sagres overflows in summer with tassel-haired youngsters armed with surfboards and a joie de vivre. The small harbour town is an excellent base from which to explore the fine beaches spread along the Algarve's untamed west coast. The sand-blown town itself is compact and crammed with welcoming pensões *and* residenciais *(bed and breakfast accommodation). This is the most south-westerly community in continental Europe, and the sense of isolation is a major part of its appeal.*

Fisherman on Sagres harbour

The Fortaleza do Beliche has two double rooms, but you must book months in advance (282) 624 124.

Try Dromedário bistro-bar on Rua Infante Dom Henrique for a mid-morning bite, or Café-Restaurante Cochina on Praça da República. On the road to Cabo de São Vicente, O Vigia has tasty home-made snacks and is a meeting point for ornithologists.

Map B6 • Tourist information office is about 1 km (0.5 mile) from the fishing harbour • (282) 624 873

Top 10 Sights

1. Fortaleza de Sagres
2. Nossa Senhora da Graça
3. Rosa dos Ventos
4. Ponta de Sagres Panoramic Walk
5. Parque Natural do Sudoeste Alentejano e Costa Vicentina
6. Cabo de São Vicente
7. Fortaleza do Beliche
8. Fortaleza da Baleeira
9. Roman Kiln Ruins
10. Menhir Circuit

1 Fortaleza de Sagres

Ominous, stark and in its time virtually impregnable, the massive front walls and two solid bastions are the impressive features of this 18th-century fort *(above; see also p53)*. Little else resembles a defensive structure today, except for the mighty cliffs themselves.

2 Nossa Senhora da Graça

The foundations of this graceful 16th-century chapel are said to have been laid by Prince Henry the Navigator *(see box)*. Its whitewashed form faces Cabo de São Vicente.

Crab pots, Sagres harbour

3 Rosa dos Ventos

The extraordinary giant wind rose, or wind compass – a device used for measuring the direction of the wind – is believed to have been built for Prince Henry *(see box)*. An impressive 43 m (141 ft) in diameter, the outline of the intriguing circle and its radiating points have been marked by pebbles *(below)*.

4 Ponta de Sagres Panoramic Walk

A bracing walk can be enjoyed round the edge of the promontory. Next to the lighthouse is a vast blow hole where you can hear the pounding of the ocean as it crashes into the rocks far below.

5 Parque Natural do Sudoeste Alentejano e Costa Vicentina

This park's wild and beautiful boundaries encompass nearly the entire western Algarve's rugged coastline and serve to protect a complex ecosystem. The area also lies under a busy migratory flight path and is popular with bird-watchers and voracious peregrine falcons *(see also p92)*.

6 Cabo de São Vicente

The forbidding look of this windblown cape is quite awe-inspiring. Greek historian Strabo, writing at the time of Christ, believed it to be the end "of all the inhabited earth", and its austere cliff face seems to encourage such thoughts *(see also p91)*.

7 Fortaleza do Beliche

Perched vertiginously on a pinnacle overlooking the Atlantic Ocean, this 17th-century fort hugs a small chapel, which in turn marks the site of the ruined Igreja de Santa Catarina. There's also a wonderfully atmospheric restaurant here.

8 Fortaleza da Baleeira

A crumbling wall and arch *(below)* are about all that remain of the harbour fortification, but the coastal view from the headland is superb.

9 Roman Kiln Ruins

Excavations near this cove at Martinhal, 2 km (1 mile) southwest of Sagres, have revealed enough Roman pottery kilns to suggest a prominent settlement. The kilns are still visible, but natural erosion has sent many tumbling seaward.

10 Menhir Circuit

Starting near Monte dos Amantes, this 2-km (1-mile) circular walk passes a series of *menhirs*, or megaliths, monumental stones that date back to 3000 BC.

Henry the Navigator (1394–1460)

Brooding, scholarly and devout, Prince Henry brought together the most learned of astronomers and astrologers, skilled cartographers and geographers, and the very best boat designers to create a school of navigation known as Vila do Infante. He oversaw and sponsored many a perilous expedition, and his vision and dedication eventually mapped the way for Portugal's "Golden Age of Discoveries".

Top 10 Albufeira

Albufeira is one of Portugal's most popular holiday destinations and the largest resort in the Algarve. Famed for its fabulous beaches and exhilarating nightlife, the town gets very busy in summer when it positively bursts with energy. Its history is just as animated, from Roman settlement 2,000 years ago, Arab and Christian conquest in the 8th and 13th centuries, respectively, its rise and fall as a centre of trade and the emergence of its fishing industry.

The café-lined streets of Albufeira

Albufeira is at its most colourful during the Festa da Ourada, a delightful festival in mid-August that takes place on the beach in honour of the patron saint of fishermen.

Albufeira is awash with bars and cafés, but particularly appealing are those lining Largo Cais Herculano. Try out Cabana Fresca, right in front of Praia dos Barcos, for their seafood snacks and chilled wine. Tasca do Viegas is another good choice.

Map G5 • Tourist Information office on Rua 5 de Outubro 8 • (289) 585 279

Top 10 Sights

1. Praia dos Barcos
2. Praia da Oura
3. Igreja de São Sebastião
4. Museu Arqueológico
5. Capela da Misericórdia
6. Tapete Mágico Crafts Workshop
7. Castle Walls
8. Igreja da Matriz
9. Galeria Pintor Samora Barros
10. "The Strip"

1 Praia dos Barcos

"Beach of the Boats" is so-named because of the many small fishing vessels left stranded on the sand between use. Their owners – grizzled fishermen with the past etched into their faces – seem oblivious to the sunbathers who descend on this well-known beach during the summer.

2 Praia da Oura

Albufeira's "Golden Beach" sweeps the toes of the village-resort of the same name. This popular beach has the advantage of its proximity to shops and cafés.

Praia dos Barcos

3 Igreja de São Sebastião

The altarpiece is the shining star of this exquisite church *(below)*. Its gilded form presides over a 14th-century statue of Nossa Senhora da Orada clutching a baby Jesus.

4 Museu Arqueológico

Peer closely and you'll spy some charming exhibits: Roman earrings; a pair of Moorish scissors unearthed at nearby Paderne castle; and a near-mint 7th-century Visigoth earthenware wine goblet. *(See p45)*

5 Capela da Misericórdia

This is Albufeira's oldest building of note. Fashioned in Gothic style in the 1500s, the chapel has since undergone many a stylistic change of heart.

6 Tapete Mágico Crafts Workshop

The quality woven table cloths, carpets and table mats for sale here are all skilfully crafted by mentally and physically disabled workers, trained in the use of a traditional, hand-operated loom. Staff are happy to show visitors around the workshops.

7 Castle Walls

The mighty ramparts that once surrounded Albufeira crumbled to dust as the 1755 Earthquake struck. A corner wall, the North Door, does survive though, in Rua Joaquim Pedro Samora. So does a remnant of St Anne's Gate, which forms part of a restaurant interior today.

8 Igreja da Matriz

Consecrated in 1800, this parish church replaces one destroyed by the Great Earthquake of 1755. The most striking feature of the present building is its imposing belltower, added in 1869 to house a carillon of eight bells.

9 Galeria Pintor Samora Barros

Named in honour of the artist/poet whose diligent handiwork adorns the church, this airy gallery *(right)* overlooking the town square stages work by contemporary Portuguese and international artists.

10 "The Strip"

Glitzy, gaudy and totally irresistible, this is Albufeira's mini Las Vegas: a narrow, neon-lit runway of hotels and restaurants, pubs, cafés and dj-bars, with the odd *artesanto* (craft shop) squeezed in. Two of the region's top nightclubs, Kiss and Liberto's, hold court here.

Water Sports

The crystal-clear waters of the Atlantic afford the Algarve a thriving water sports scene. At its simplest, fun begins with the humble pedalo, but for the more sea-hardy there's a subaqua school at Praia da Oura, where seasoned divers rub fins with less-experienced snorkellers. Praia da Galé, about 6 km (3 miles) west, is a fashionable centre for jet- and water-skiing, while windsurfers make for Falésia. The wind can whip up a treat at Praia da Falésia, so it is also the favoured launch pad for paragliders.

For more on Albufeira's attractions and nightlife **See pp 62, 71, 77, 80 and 81**

TOP 10 Vila Real and Castro Marim

The original fishing village of Vila Real de Santo António was wiped out at the beginning of the 17th century by a momentous tidal surge. It wasn't until 1773 that Vila Real regained a place on the map. The town's reconstruction was overseen by the Marquês de Pombal (1699–1782), and under his eye the new town was planned and built, making use of a unique grid system. The town attracts day-trippers from Spain, and visitors can easily take in nearby Castro Marim, too.

Colourful houses, Vila Real

When searching for Reserva Natural do Sapal en route from Castro Marim, look out for a small sign on the right with "Sede" written next to a blue and white logo of an avocet wading bird.

Café Cantinho do Marquês, Praça Marquês de Pombal, 24, is a cheerful and accommodating bar which looks out onto Vila Real's central square.

Map P3–4 • Castro Marim is 5 km (3 miles) north of Vila Real • Vila Real Tourist Information, Centro Cultural António Aleixo, Rua Teófilo de Braga • (281) 542 100 • Castro Marim Tourist Information, Rua José Alves Moreira 2/4 • (281) 531 232

Top 10 Sights

1. Praça Marquês de Pombal
2. Museu Manuel Cabanas
3. Igreja Matriz
4. Castro Marim
5. Igreja de Santiago
6. Museu Arqueológico
7. Former Igreja da Misericórdia
8. Fortaleza São Sebastião
9. Reserva Natural do Sapal
10. Medieval Fair

1 Praça Marquês de Pombal

Vila Real's handsome central square is named after its creator, the Marquês de Pombal, and features a boldly graphic black and white mosaic pavement radiating from a central obelisk. The square is lined by a row of orange trees, which bear plump fruit, and a number of tidy 18th-century town houses, cafés and restaurants.

2 Museu Manuel Cabanas

Dedicated to Portugal's foremost wood engraver, this museum ably spotlights Cabanas' extensive portfolio of ink-relief images. *(See also p45)*

Praça Marquês de Pombal

3 Igreja Matriz

The highpoint, literally, of a visit to this church *(below)* is its six gorgeous stained-glass windows, set aloft over the chapel and altar. They were designed and installed by Algarvean artist Joaquim Rebocho as part of a major restoration in 1949. A further set at ground-floor level floods the baptistery with a surreal rainbow glow.

4 Castro Marim

This brooding frontier stronghold *(above)* consists of two castles. The inner part, built by Dom Alfonso III in the 13th century, became headquarters of the Order of Christ. Dom João IV added heavier outer ramparts in the 17th century.

5 Igreja de Santiago

Surrounded by a jumble of masonry, a cracked but intact portal with a damaged stone crucifix crowning its arch is the most tangible evidence of the Igreja de Santiago, where Henry the Navigator once prayed.

6 Museu Arqueológico

Tucked inside the weather-worn battlements of Castro Marim castle is a humble museum, displaying a collection of local finds, including ancient lances, chipped cannon balls, ceramic fragments and amphorae. (Currently closed for renovation.)

7 Former Igreja da Misericórdia

Replaced many years ago by a much larger church situated outside the castle walls, the original 17th-century church *(above)* has still kept its looks thanks to generous restoration work. Unfortunately, you cannot see much beyond the Renaissance doorway as the church is closed to the public.

8 Fortaleza São Sebastião

Mirroring Castro Marim's castle from a nearby hilltop, this smaller fort was built for Dom João IV in 1641. Now in ruins, the fort is redeemed by its panoramic views.

9 Reserva Natural do Sapal

A large expanse of marsh and salt pans that is an important breeding ground for plovers, avocets, little terns and black-winged stilts. Flamingos may also be seen feeding here.

10 Medieval Fair

Swordsmen, archers and jousters battle it out under the illuminated walls of the castle, as Castro Marim celebrates its medieval past through pageantry. The raucous period fun goes on for three days *(see p58)*.

The Salt Industry

Traditional saltworks like those near the centre of Castro Marim are made up of shallow reservoirs, or pans. Set below sea level, the pans are subdivided into small ponds called *talhos*, into which salt water flows. The water evaporates in the heat of the sun, and the salt crystalizes. The process is repeated over a number of weeks until enough has been deposited. It's then removed onto the mud walls (*barachas*) that divide each pan, where it is collected into huge pyramids, for the most part using manual labour.

Left **Roman fish mosaic** Right **Painting of the Great Earthquake of 1755**

Top 10 Moments in History

1 3000 BC: Early Peoples and Trade

Stone burial chambers (dolmens) and *menhirs* are characteristic of this period. By 1000 BC, Phoenicians have established sizeable trading stations. The Greeks also come, but their trade links are severed by the Carthaginians who blockade the Straits of Gibraltar and in 550 BC found the city of Portus Hannibalis (Portimão).

Menhir of Almendres

2 218–202 BC: Second Punic War

The Romans defeat the Carthaginians, then sweep through the Iberian peninsula. During the next 400 years, grand Roman cities and luxurious villas sprout up.

3 AD 415: Visigoths

After the fall of the Roman Empire the reins of power are seized by the Visigoths, a formidable warrior caste from eastern France and Germany.

4 711: The Moors Arrive

Internal strife and persecution among the Visigoths ultimately leads to one faction appealing for aid from Muslim North Africa. A large army of Berbers and Arabs conquers huge swathes of the Iberian peninsula. The Moors dominate the Algarve for well over 500 years, giving the region its name, al-Gharb, and turning Silves into an intellectual hub of staggering opulence.

Henry the Navigator

5 Christian Crusades

Though Christians reconquer central Portugal in the 12th century, the Algarve is still firmly under Moorish rule. Dom Sancho (1185–1211) briefly takes Silves in 1189, but the city is recaptured by Al-Mansur. Dom Sancho II (1223–48) later launches a campaign to invade southern Portugal with the help of northern European Crusaders.

6 Portugal is Born

Faro is the last Moorish stronghold to fall, in 1249. Portuguese sovereignty over the Algarve is confirmed in a treaty with the kingdom of Castile in 1297.

7 Era of the Great Discoveries

The Algarve plays a pivotal role in Portugal's maritime expansion in the 15th century. Henry the Navigator is made governor of the Algarve in 1418 and initiates the voyages

Tanks rolling in during the 1974 coup

of discovery from his bases in Sagres and Lagos. By the time of his death in 1460, Madeira, the Azores and Cape Verde islands have been discovered and much of the west coast of Africa has been mapped. In 1488 Bartolomeu Dias rounds the Cape of Good Hope, and ten years later Vasco da Gama opens the trade route to India.

8 Artistic Extravagance
The discovery of gold and diamonds in Brazil during the reign of Pedro II (1683–1706) later finances a period of great artistic extravagance under João V, who rules until 1750.

9 Great Earthquake of 1755
The quake devastates Lisbon and much of southern Portugal and plunges the nation into long-lasting crisis. Napoleon's troops invade in 1807.

10 Republicanism and Integration with Europe
The late 19th century witnesses political strife, with Republicanism taking root. António de Oliveira Salazar becomes prime minister in 1932, and turns around a stagnating economy but with the sacrifice of democracy. The army overthrows the government in 1974 in a near-bloodless coup. On 1 January 2002 the country adopts the euro currency.

Myths and Legends

1 The Moorish King and the Nordic Princess
The mythical king planted 1000s of almond trees to convince the princess that the blossom was like the snow she was used to.

2 Henry the Navigator
Henry assembled the best nautical minds in an academy, but why is there no trace of it?

3 Curse of the Vixen
On stormy nights in the Algarve hinterland, the raucous bellows of a hideous beast can be heard.

4 Capture of Aljezur Castle, 1249
A maid may have prevented the capture, but mistook the attacking knights for Moorish defenders and failed to raise the alarm.

5 St Vincent
Cabo de Sào Vicente is associated with a 4th-century martyr, whose body was watched over by ten ravens.

6 Enchanted Cássima
The pitiful cries of a Moorish woman supposedly echo in the streets near Loulé Castle.

7 Hannibal and the Elephants
Legend has it that the great general landed at Portimão.

8 Manueline Window
King Dom Sebastião (1557–78) is said to have roused an army from the window at Lagos Castle.

9 Pot of Treasure
A pot full of gold coins lies on the road between Mexilhoeira Grande and Praia da Rocha. Kiss the toad guarding it, and the pot is yours.

10 The Cry of Aben Afen
Listen out for battle cries near Silves – the ghost of the city's last Arab lord.

Left **Sunbathers** Centre **Rocky outcrops, São Rafael** Right **Children, Praia da Rocha**

TOP 10 Beaches

1 Praia da Dona Ana, Lagos

A beautiful and intimate beach, caressed by clear waters and flanked by huge outcrops of mustard-red sandstone. Easily reached by car and public transport, and about 25 minutes' walk from the centre of Lagos. A nearby warren of coves and hidden grottoes is ripe for exploration by boat. *Map D5*

2 Praia da Ilha de Tavira, Tavira

Ostensibly an elongated sand bar, Ilha de Tavira's windward side is a magnet for water sports enthusiasts. Leeward, opposite Tavira, the sheltered beach skirts a campsite and a string of cafés and fine seafood restaurants. There are two access points to this spit. From Pedras del Rei, you can walk across a causeway or catch a ride on a miniature railway. Alternatively, regular ferry boats depart from the jetty at Quatro Águas. *Map M5*

3 Praia dos Barcos, Albufeira

This hugely popular tract of sand is characterized by the colourful fishing boats stationed at one end – indeed, Praia dos Barcos is also known as "Fisherman's Beach". Right in front of the town's old quarter, the beach is reached through a tunnel next to the tourist information office. *Map G5*

4 Praia do Armado, Carrapateira

Pummelled by Atlantic swells, Armado is one of Portugal's premier surfing venues, and its surf school enjoys international patronage. Sitting well off the beaten track, this west coast beach also attracts families, and the rock pools at low tide teem with inquisitive children. *Map B4*

5 Praia da Rocha, Portimão

One of the most famous and impressive beaches in the Algarve, Praia da Rocha is one vast blanket of golden sand set against a backdrop of cliffs the colour of cinnamon. It can get very crowded in summer, but a tunnel at the western end allows access to narrower stretches of sand. At various points along Avenida Tómas Cabreira there is further access via steps, some of them steep. *Map E5*

Praia da Dona Ana

Praia da São Rafael

6 Praia da São Rafael, Albufeira

With its shallow waters and soft white sand, Praia da São Rafael can fill up quickly. Its pretty bay is framed by some extraordinary rock formations, pocked by a number of caves just waiting to be investigated. It offers ideal snorkelling territory and is popular with families. *Map G5*

7 Praia de Odeceixe

One of the Algarve's best kept secrets, Odeceixe is in a spectacular setting, up in the northwest corner of the Algarve. Its sheltered, crescent-shaped beach is just a short drive (along a road that shadows the path of the river) from the quaint village of Odeceixe. Even in summer, the beach is always wonderfully uncrowded. *Map C1*

8 Praia da Marinha, Benagil

Steep steps hewn into rock lead down to two compact and secluded beaches tucked below soaring cliffs. A treat for snorkellers, Marinha is served by a small café. *Map F5*

9 Praia de Figueira, Salema

This select swathe of sand is popular with youngsters and windsurfers. There are also some excellent nearby dive sites, such as Boco do Rio to the east, where the wreck of the *Ocean*, an 18th-century French man-of-war, lies in shallow water. Praia de Figueira lies right in front of the village of Salema. Arrive early to find parking space. *Map C5*

Praia de Odeceixe

10 Meia Praia, Lagos

A giant curve of sand 4 km (2 miles) in length makes this the longest beach in the Algarve. There's plenty of room for water-skiing, windsurfing and jet-skiing and those seeking a little peace and quiet. It also makes for a lovely walk, especially in autumn when the summer hoards have begun to disperse. *Map D5*

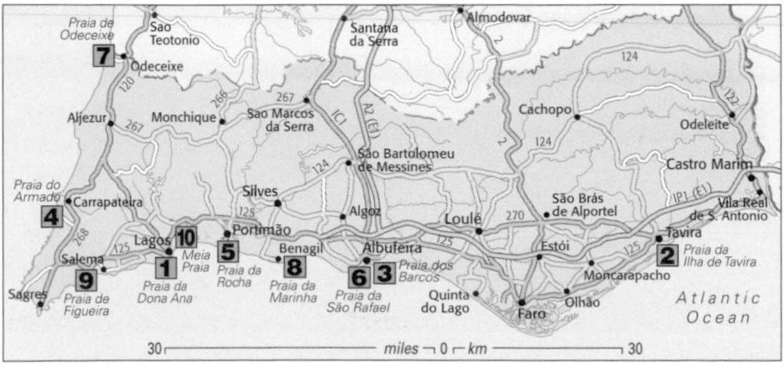

Left **Monte Gordo** Right **Carvoeiro**

TOP 10 Resort Towns

1 Lagos
Drawing the whole gamut of visitors, from backpackers, package tourists and wealthy expatriates, Lagos exudes a lively and inviting atmosphere. Modern amenities and historical sights make for an appealing mix of old and new, and the nearby coves, framed by russet and mustard rocky outcrops, are some of the most spectacular in the Algarve *(see pp20–21)*. *Map D5*

2 Albufeira
Bright, loud and unashamedly extrovert, Albufeira buzzes with vitality in summer. Wide sweeping beaches, first-class water sport facilities and dozens of bars, bistros, restaurants and nightclubs lend the resort its non-stop party atmosphere, though the old quarter still manages to convey a mellow charm. *(See pp30–31.)* *Map G5*

3 Praia da Rocha
Some of the very first holiday hotels in the Algarve sprang up here back in the 1960s, and Praia da Rocha hasn't looked back since. Vibrant and engaging, this resort is famed for its outstanding golden beach. And at night, revellers dance till dawn in the clubs and bars that skirt the sand. *Map E5*

4 Vilamoura
Designed around a marina of international repute, this upmarket resort has championship golf courses, a stylish casino, luxury hotels and sumptuous villas. Fabulous cruises depart from the marina *(see p72)*. *Map H5*

5 Alvor
Nestling in a sheltered bay midway between Portimão and Lagos, Alvor is an unusual mix of dignified charm and flickering

Albufeira

neon. The old quarter is a delight to wander through, the 16th-century Manueline church is a gem and the village restaurants serve up some of the tastiest seafood in the region. ⊗ *Map D4*

6 Armação de Pêra

The beach here is one of the longest in the Algarve and fronts a commercial hub of tall, angular apartment blocks, seafront hotels and rows of cafés and bistro bars. But this is all rather functional, so instead everyone heads east for Pêra's livelier old town, spread around the site of a small fortress. ⊗ *Map F5*

7 Carvoeiro

Friendliness suffuses this alluring little town, making it ideal for families. It is one of the Algarve's main self-catering areas, and the hilltops that flank the pocket-sized beach are awash with apartments. On the other side of the promontory is the snorkelling territory of Algar Seco rock formation. ⊗ *Map E5*

8 Monte Gordo

A generous beach and a casino (Casino Monte Gordo, 8900 Monte Gordo) are the twin targets for most visitors to this, the closest Algarve beach resort to the Spanish border. The esplanade is fringed by lofty palms and even loftier apartment blocks with fabulous views of the ocean. ⊗ *Map P4*

Armação de Pêra

9 Sagres

Though not strictly a resort town – it has little in the way of entertainment infrastructure and its isolated position keeps it off the tourist treadmill – Sagres offers access to some of the most unspoilt beaches in the Algarve. *(See pp28–9.)* ⊗ *Map B6*

10 Quarteira

The brazen tourist hub that is Quarteira is home to a throng of holiday apartments near the beach. The remodelled fishing harbour is a hive of activity in the mornings, when returning boats deposit their glistening catch on the quayside, most of it destined for the town's market next door. ⊗ *Map H5*

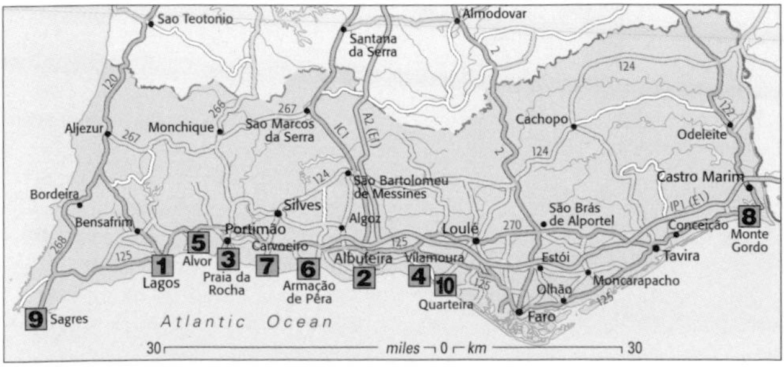

Left **View across the river from Alcoutim** Right **Caldas de Monchique**

Inland Villages

1 Alte

The town's cobbled streets, colourful window frames and cheerful chimney pots invoke an unhurried air that is quite disarming. Alte's church retains a fine portal and is situated near a leafy square. The spring running along its flank tumbles under an old mill, providing a favourite picnic spot. *Map H3*

2 Caldas de Monchique

The warm spa water here has brought visitors since at least the age of the Roman Empire. It is just as alluring today, but there are other reasons to visit this hillside hamlet, not least the wood of pine and eucalyptus which provides a lush, cooling canopy in the heat of summer. Woodsmoke and birdsong drift lazily through a valley peppered with whitewashed cottages and smallholdings. *Map E3*

Alte

3 Alcoutim

The town's 14th-century castle keeps one timeworn eye on its townsfolk and the other on the old adversary, Sanlúcar, Alcoutim's mirror image on the Spanish side of the River Guadiana. The silence here is palpable, interrupted only by the chiming hour and the rattle of stork bills as they chatter to one another from church towers and chimney stacks. *Map P1*

4 Estói

Just off the town's main square is the Palácio do Visconde de Estói, a 19th-century Rococo palace, with gardens fanned by giant palms and cooled by fountains. A ten-minute walk from here brings you to the site of Milreu, a Roman complex dominated by the apse of a temple that was converted into a Christian basilica in the 5th century. *Map K5 • Palace Tue–Sat, free • Milreu Tue–Sun, Adm*

5 Salir

The walls of Salir's Moorish castle are lit up at night and emit an eerie glow, but on the other side of the village the view is more benign, stretching across the valley from the parish church and garden. In summer this rural idyll is blanketed by narcissi and alive with the warbling of brightly coloured passerines. *Map J3*

Salir

6 Paderne

Early in the 17th century the entire population of Paderne moved from the shadows of the nearby castle to the environs of a newly consecrated church. That village is now a sleepy place of faded charm and modest means, but therein lies its beauty. The architecture retains a certain grandeur, while the Moorish castle stands close by, still wondering where all the people went. *Map G4*

7 Querença

Querença is the focus of some attention in January when the village hosts its annual *festa das chouriças* (sausage festival, *see p59*). For the rest of the year Querença is rather quiet – an isolated but attractive settlement surrounded by the Caldeirão mountain range. *Map K4*

Village sign, Querença

8 Guerreiros do Rio

The scenic road south from Alcoutim runs part way along the banks of the River Guadiana and passes through a landscape bristling with olive, fig and carob trees before reaching this tiny village. Amid the orange trees, a former schoolhouse now houses a modest museum that provides an interesting glimpse into the history of the Guadiana River. *Map P2*

9 Martin Longo

The storks nesting on top of the belfry of Martin Longo's parish church have been members of this small community for years, and they are as appealing as their unusual home. But the "A Flor da Agulha" dolls workshop is also worth a visit, for it is here that traditional jute dolls are hand crafted, the figurines depicting ladies spinning, herdsmen and woodmen. *Map L1*

10 Barão de São João

Wrapped in classic hill-walking country and pleasantly lost in time, Barão de São João typifies rural Algarve. It is best appreciated during the antiques fair, which the village hosts on the last Sunday of every month. *Map C4*

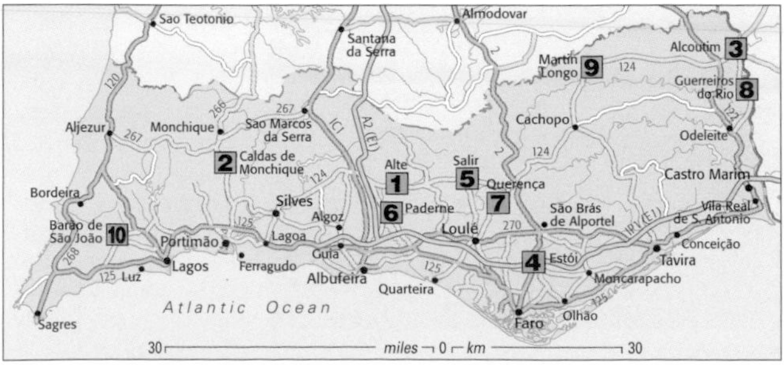

Left **Fishermen's cottages, Cacelha Velha** Centre **Surfer near Arrifana** Right **Salema beach**

Top 10 Coastal Villages

1 Cacelha Velha

The settlement is little more than a whitewashed church, a squat, 18th-century fortress and a row of fishermen's cottages, but it is quite exquisite and totally unspoilt. Fanned by an invigorating sea breeze, this smudge of antiquity looks out over a lagoon and the Atlantic beyond. It's a popular weekend destination for locals, who are happy to queue for the only restaurant. *Map N4*

2 Ferragudo

A maze of cottages, converted lofts and cube-like town houses tumble down towards the river and Praia Grande, a vast swathe of sand popular with sunbathers and windsurfers. The seafood restaurants lining the tidy quayside are some of the best in the Algarve. *Map E5*

3 Santa Luzia

An old seafaring myth claims Santa Luzia came by its foreign-sounding name after an effigy of the Virgin Mary was salvaged from an Italian vessel. Today the image most associated with Santa Luzia is *covos* – octopus pots. This is the octopus capital of the Algarve, and hundreds of the earthenware pots, all numbered and roped together, can be found piled neatly on the beach in readiness for their next outing. *Map M5*

4 Salema

Even if you're not staying in Salema, it's worth detouring to it from the EN 125, via the beautiful ravine, speckled most of the year with colourful flora and fleet-footed goats. The tarmac peters out where the cobbled slip road begins, a causeway cluttered with colourful fishing boats, rickety lobster pots and shrouds of netting. The sloping streets are banked with salt-laced terraced houses and cramped little tavernas. *Map C5*

Santa Luzia

5 Burgau

The best time to savour the village-like atmosphere of Burgau is out of season. You notice more when the cobbled lanes are deserted and the only sound is the collision of the ocean with the beach. There are some lovely coastal walks, too, with many prime picnic spots. *Map C5*

6 Odeceixe

The isolated splendour of this attractive hillside village makes the long drive north along the Algarve's western coast worthwhile. Odeceixe's beach, cut in two by the mouth of the Seixe creek, is the prize draw *(see p37)*. Late spring is the best time of year to visit, when it's warm and not too busy. ⊗ *Map C1*

7 Carrapateira

This is where surfers come to relax after a day taming the waves at Praia da Bordeira and Praia do Armado *(see p36)*. A loose configuration of terraced cottages and sandblown cafés, Carrapateira is well used to the camper vans that disgorge the salt-encrusted youths. ⊗ *Map B4*

8 Arrifana

Craggy, precipitous cliffs tower over Arrifana's superb beach and accompanying village, which looks as though it's about to be swallowed up by the dunes. This is the west coast at its wildest and most desolate, attracting only die-hard surfers and those seeking solace with the elements. ⊗ *Map B3*

Odeceixe

Benagil

9 Benagil

Benagil straddles a steep, narrow valley which ambles its way towards a bay the size of a postage stamp. More hamlet than village, Benagil is blessed with a couple of superb seafood restaurants positioned on the lip of the valley, with views across the ocean. ⊗ *Map F5*

10 Luz de Tavira

It's one of those villages you normally drive through on your way somewhere else. But stop off to view the south door of the local church. The highly ornate portal is one of the loveliest examples of Manueline architecture in the Algarve. ⊗ *Map M5*

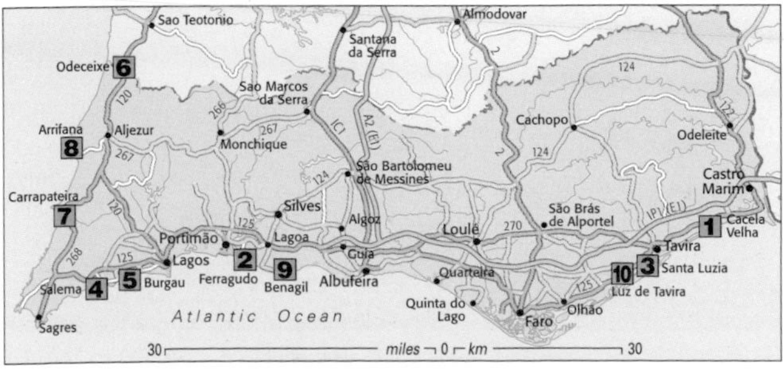

Left **Mosaic, Museu Arqueológico, Albufeira** Right **Museu da Cortiça, Silves**

Top 10 Museums

1 Museu Regional, Lagos

This highly entertaining ethnographic museum brings together a fantastic collection of oddities, rarities and priceless treasures *(see pp22–3)*.

2 Museu Arqueológico, Faro

Set within the cloisters of the former convent of Nossa Senhora da Assunção, this museum is one of the most beautiful in the Algarve. A giant Roman floor mosaic, fragments of a Moorish bowl inscribed with "Allah" and a gallery devoted to 16th-century Italian paintings are just some of the highlights.

Largo Dom Afonso III • Map K6 • 10am–6pm Tue & Fri, 2.30pm–6pm Mon, Wed, Thu & Sat (times may vary slightly in winter) • Adm

3 Museu Cerro da Vila, Vilamoura

A first-rate modern museum and historic Roman site rolled into one, Cerro da Vila is an outstanding example of a 2nd-century villa complex, complete with sunken baths, salt tanks, a burial tower and brilliant black-and-white patterned mosaics. The adjacent museum houses a superb display of Roman, Visigoth and Moorish artifacts.

Cerro da Vila • Map H5 • 10am–1pm, 4pm–9pm daily • Adm

4 Museu Arqueológico, Silves

This excellent museum is unique in Portugal for its astonishing 12th-century Arab well-cistern. Unearthed by chance in 1980, it is the star exhibit around which the entire building is constructed. An original staircase (closed to the public) incorporated into the ancient structure descends 15 m (49 ft) to the bottom of the well.

Rua das Portas de Loulé • Map F4 • 10am–6pm Tue–Sun • Adm

5 Museu Etnográfico do Trajo Algarvio, São Brás de Alportel

This delightful rural ensemble of local costumes, papier-mâché dolls, decorated carriages and

Left **Museu Arqueológico, Faro** Right **Museu Arqueológico, Silves**

Museu Etnográfico do Trajo Algarvio

traditional handicraft is aptly housed in a wonderful country mansion. Particularly poignant is a child's faded tunic and breeches displayed next to a photograph of one José Maria Féria wearing the same costume in 1929. *Rua Dr José Dias Sancho • Map K4 • 10am–1pm & 2pm–5pm Mon–Fri, 2pm–5pm Sat & Sun • Adm*

6 Museu da Cortiça, Silves

Silves' cork museum and factory highlights the impact this abundant and versatile bark has had on the town through a series of huge photographic panels, themed exhibitions and displays of early 20th-century machinery housed in converted workshops. *Rua Gregório Mascarenhas • Map F4 • 282 440 440 for group bookings with guide • 9.30am–12.45pm & 2pm–9.45pm (6pm winter) daily • Adm*

7 Museu Municipal, Loulé

Loulé's archaeological heritage is admirably chronicled with displays of Stone Age, Bronze Age and Roman artifacts. Upstairs, history is closer to the present day, with a reconstruction of a traditional Algarve kitchen, replete with 19th-century crockery and a worn *xarém*, or maize wheel. *7 Rua D. Paio Peres Correia • Map J4 • 9am–5.30pm Mon–Fri, 10am–2pm Sat • Adm*

8 Museu Marítimo, Faro

Carlos Porfirio's dramatic oil painting of wild-eyed fishermen drawing a huge net over a shoal of desperate, thrashing tuna overlooks this spirited exhibition of nautical paraphernalia. The scale models of caravels, galleons and steamboats are wonderful. *Rua da Comunidade Lusiada • Map K6 • 2pm–4pm Mon–Fri • Adm*

9 Museu Arqueológico, Albufeira

The view from the this modern museum looks out to the ocean, while inside is a modest but fascinating collection of Stone Age, Roman and Moorish artifacts. The 10th-century Arab silo is worth close scrutiny, as are the set of weathered 16th-century keystones. *1 Praça da República, Albufeira • Map G5 • 2.30pm–8pm Mon–Sat (10.30am–5pm in winter) • Free*

10 Museu Manuel Cabanas, Vila Real de Santo António

A museum showcasing the work of Portugal's greatest wood engraver of the 20th century, Manuel Cabanas (1902–95). A truly dynamic volume of work is exhibited: ink-relief images of politicians, statesmen, writers and musicians, plus views of everyday rural life. *António Aleixo cultural centre, Rua Dr Teófilo Braga, Vila Real de Santo António • Map P4 • 10.30am–12.30pm & 3pm–7pm daily; 4pm–8pm & 9pm–11pm (15 Jul–15 Sep) • Free*

Museu Marítimo, Faro

Left **San Lorenzo** Centre **Le Meridien Penina Hotel** Right **Pinta Course**

TOP 10 Premier Golf Courses

1 San Lorenzo

In the Parque Natural da Ria Formosa and one of the top five golf courses in continental Europe. The par 72 layout culminates with a green on the 18th that must be approached from across a lake. Owned by the nearby Le Meridien Dona Filipa Hotel *(see p122)*, the course is open to visitors, although priority is given to hotel guests. *San Lorenzo Golf Club, Quinta do Lago, Almansil • Map J5*

2 Penina Championship Course

A par 73 layout designed by the great golf-course architect Sir Henry Cotton in the mid-1960s. Le Meridien Penina hotel *(see p122)* overlooks the course, which stretches over parkland terrain, its sweeping fairways dotted by water hazards. Two of the great holes are the dogleg 5th, with its canal, lake and contoured green, and the alarming 13th, shadowed by water from tee to green. *Apartado 146 Penina, Portimão • Map E4*

3 Quinta do Lago

This par 72 championship course lying within the vast estate of the same name has hosted the Portuguese Open on several occasions. The undulating layout favours long hitters, but strategic bunkering, the odd water hazard and large, contoured greens provide challenge aplenty. *Quinta do Lago Campo de Golfe, Quinta do Lago, Almancil • Map J5*

4 Sheraton Pine Cliffs

A spectacular clifftop layout, this 9-hole course is set against an ocean backdrop. The course hides under a canopy of umbrella pine, with narrow fairways demanding a steady swing. The final hole requires a shot from the clifftop tee that will carry a deep ravine to hit the green. *Pine Cliffs, Praia da Falésia – Apartado 644, Albufeira • Map G5*

Sheraton Pine Cliffs

5 Royal Course, Vale do Lobo

A rolling terrain abundant with pine envelopes this par 72 layout. The highlight is the infamous 16th, where a powerful and accurate swing is needed to carry a set of precipitous cliffs before the green. But the signature hole is the 9th, with its spectacular, semi-island green. *Royal Golf Course, Vale do Lobo, Vale do Lobo • Map J5*

6 The Old Course, Vilamoura

A mature course of classic British design, opened in 1969 and still revered today. Endowed with mostly narrow, pine tree-lined fairways, the only lake is on the 4th, where the tee shot must clear not only the water but also a large pine and bunker hugging the green. *The Old Course, Clube de Golfe, Vilamoura • Map H5*

7 Pinta Course, Pestana Carvoeiro

One of the layout's wonders is a stately olive tree, believed to be over 1,200 years old. In fact, most of the natural contours of this par 71 estate were retained to include the ancient tree life that characterizes this course. Pinta is home to the prestigious David Leadbetter Academy. *Pinta Course, Pinta Pestana Golf & Resort, Apartado 1011, Carvoeiro LGA • Map E5*

8 Pinheiro Altos

This par 72 is very much of two halves. The outward nine snake lazily through lofty pine wood, while the back nine skirt some daunting water hazards. The course falls within the Ria Formosa nature reserve, making it an especially attractive course. *Pinheiros Altos, Quinta do Lago, 135 Almansil • Map J5*

Pinheiro Altos

9 Parque da Floresta

Built on hilly coastal terrain, this challenging par 72 can be exposed to stiff breezes, so club selection can vary considerably in the unpredictable winds. Never more so than on the short 5th, which is played from hilltop to the crown of a hillock. *Parque da Floresta Golf and Leisure Resort, Vale do Poço, Budens • Map C5*

10 Salgados

An inspiring coastal course that features several links holes skirting the beach, Salgados has the largest number of water hazards to be found on any Algarve course – a frightening fourteen! An additional threat is the spirited winds that whip up off the sea. *Salgados Golf Club, Apartado 2266 – Vale do Rabelho, Albufeira • Map G5*

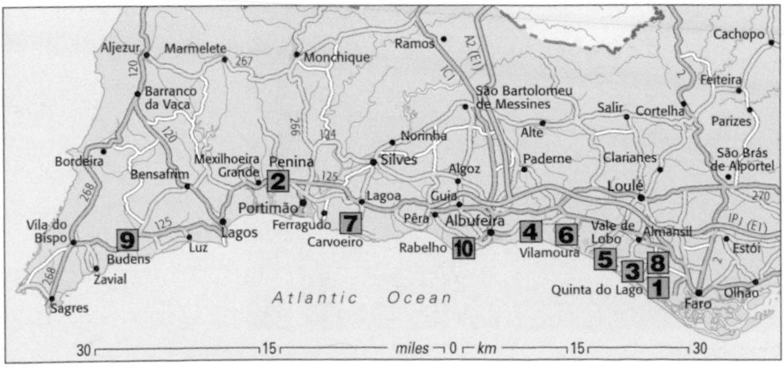

Left **Alto Golf** Centre **Benamor** Right **Vila Sol**

TOP 10 Holiday Golf Courses

1 Vale de Milho

This superb 9-hole course is a test of a golfer's short game. A compact layout of interesting holes, the design encompasses regularly sized greens, ingenious water hazards and bunkers similar to those found on a full course. First-class service and amenities include a computerized swing analysis. Ideal for combining a little golf with regular excursions to the nearby beaches. *Vale de Milho Golf, Apartado 1273 – Praia do Carvoeiro, Carvoeiro LGA • Map E5*

2 Alto Golf

With its sweeping views of the ocean, this splendid course was the last work of eminent designer Sir Henry Cotton. Over 10,000 trees were planted on the par 72 layout, attracting a wealth of colourful birdlife. Aside from the 604-m (nearly 2,000-ft) 16th, the course is not overly difficult and can be enjoyed by golfers of all standards. *Apartado 1 – Alvor • Map D5*

3 Penina Academy Course

A compact, 9-hole course laid out amid the Championship fairways. The ease of play should relax even the most nervous of players, and the adjoining golf academy offers individual or group tuition. *Penina Golf & Resort Hotel, Apartado 146 Penina, Portimão • Map E4*

4 Balaia

Popular with beginners as well as the more adroit, this new layout, opened in April 2001, is recommended for the holiday golfer who prefers a fairly relaxed game. It requires concentration, however, especially for club selection, as the holes vary in length more than one might expect of a 9-hole course. *Balaia Golf Village, Apartado 917, Sitío da Balaia, Albufeira • Map G5*

5 Benamor

A beautiful, rolling par 71 course, with widely varying holes and a mix of coastal and mountain views. The outward nine are relatively easy, but the trickiness factor picks up in the back nine, particularly on the 15th and 18th, the latter having out of bounds areas on either side close to the green. *Quinta de Benamor, Conceição, Tavira • Map M4*

Vale de Milho

6 Vila Sol

Originally a standard 18-hole course, a third 9-hole loop was introduced, allowing for three combinations of 18 holes. The course features daunting water hazards and large, contoured greens. The club also has an excellent driving range and academy. *Vila Sol, Morgadinhos Beach, Golf & Country Club, Alto do Semino, Vilamoura • Map H5*

7 Quinta da Ria

Bordering the Parque Natural da Ria Formosa, this par 72 layout affords the distraction of some spectacular ocean views. Amid olive and carob trees, some of the man-made lakes have now become home to many species of waterfowl. Elsewhere, greens skirt a vineyard and an orange grove. *Quinta da Ria, 8901 Vila Nova de Cacela • Map N4*

8 Castro Marim

The excellent par 71 Atlantic Course commands glorious views across the River Guadiana and to Spain beyond. The new layout features a number of lakes, undulating fairways and elevated greens, and has been designed to offer a challenging yet relaxing experience to golfers of all levels. *Castro Marim Golfe and Country Club, Apartado 70, Castro Marim • Map P3*

9 Gramacho Course, Pestana Carvoeiro

Gramacho has recently gained another 9-hole layout to add to the original double nine, and the combination allows for a variety of options in pin settings and length to suit both high and low handicappers. *Gramacho Course, Pestana Golf & Resort – Apartado 1011, Carvoeiro LGA • Map E5*

10 Palmares

Beaches fringing Lagos in the near-distance make this par 71 layout a year-round holiday favourite, and the course features five links holes that take you into dunes close to the ocean – a beguiling challenge. *Pamares Golf, Monte Palmares, Meia Praia, Lagos • Map D5*

Palmares

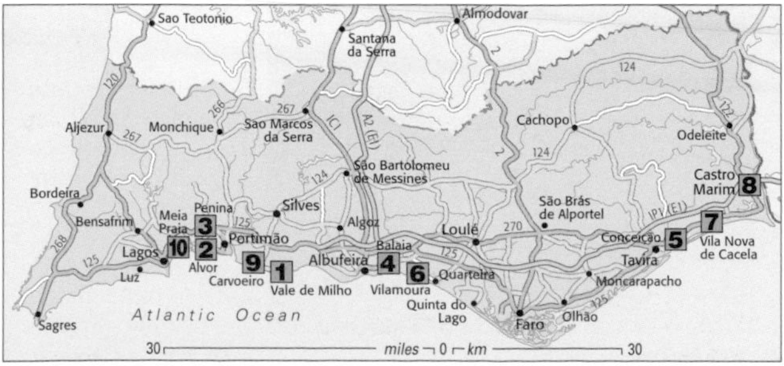

Left **Reserva Natural do Sapal nature trail** Right **Monchique-Fóia circuit**

TOP 10 Walks in the Algarve

1 Parque Natural da Ria Formosa/São Lourenço and Quinta do Lago Trails

Two one-hour nature trails reveal a rich coastal wonderland of salt marsh, woodland and freshwater lagoon. The winter months are very rewarding with huge flocks of greater flamingo and spoonbill mingling with pintail, gadwall and teal. The prize attraction, though, is the rare purple gallinule, a striking member of the coot family. *Map J–L6*

2 Tavira National Forest (Mata Nacional)

Fine, panoramic views characterize an easy to moderate walk, the start/finish point of which is only accessible by car. The 8-km (5-mile) track snakes its way through beautiful rolling countryside, fording two small streams and passing the diminutive villages of Malhada de Peres and Daroeira. *Map M4*

3 Monchique-Fóia-Monchique Circuit

The 11-km (7-mile) walk begins in the town square and takes in the ruins of a Franciscan convent. Shady woodlands echo in summer to nightingales and cuckoos, and are full of butterflies tumbling through the air. The ascent steepens before the cluster of antenna prickling Fóia's summit come into view. *Map E3*

4 Burgau Coastal Walk

The spectacular clifftop paths between Salema and Luz are well-trodden by ramblers who enjoy negotiating headlands and don't mind the occasional stony track. The full distance is about 10 km (6 miles), but to halve that length, start the walk from Burgau. *Map C5*

5 "Ilha" do Rosário, Silves

A serene circular walk which partly follows the course of an irrigation ditch *(levada)* and two rivers. The 8-km (4-mile) path begins at the Mira-Rio restaurant on the N124 where it picks up the *levada* before heading towards the "Ilha" do Rosário viewpoint. The path then veers through lush, open countryside and skirts a tiny hamlet, Vale da Lama, before meeting the restaurant again. *Map F4*

Rocha da Pena, Penina circuit

6 Reserva Natural do Sapal Nature Trail

The trail is around 6 km (3 miles) in length and two hours in duration, although ornithologists can spend all day in bliss scanning the reedbeds and saltmarsh for plovers, avocets and other wading birds, plus many species of duck and gull. During the summer, visitors can also observe the salt harvest. ✆ *Map P4*

Benagil-Senhora da Rocha Clifftop trek

7 Climb to Rocha dos Soidos, Alte

Combines exploration of Alte, arguably the prettiest village in the Algarve, with a hike to the summit of Rocha dos Soidos. The climb is long and steady rather than steep. It will take about three hours to complete the round trip which includes an alternative route of descent via Soidos de Baixo. ✆ *Map H3*

8 Esteveira Dune Walk

The fragile habitat of the dunes contains a wealth of flora, including the beautiful large yellow restharrow which blankets the sand with a bright mantle of delicate petals. ✆ *Map C2*

9 Penina Circuit

A real hike in the hills that will appeal to the experienced hill walker. The region is a protected area of outstanding natural beauty and bristles with aromatic lavender and rosemary. Native *cistus* species are the dominant shrubs. The walk passes two ancient defensive walls and the Cave of the Moors. ✆ *Map J3*

10 Benagil-Senhora da Rocha Clifftop Trek

Coastal erosion has eaten into the cliff face to produce some fantastic natural sculpture washed with a beautiful russet and mustard hue. The footpath, which is quite steep in places, looks over a series of delightful half-moon coves packed with golden sand. And there are ample spots to picnic in along the way. ✆ *Map F5*

Left **Castro Marim** Centre **Fortaleza Cacelha Velha** Right **Silves**

TOP 10 Castles and Forts

1 Silves

One of the Algarve's great landmark features, Silves Castle dates back to Moorish times, but may have been built on Roman fortifications. Its formidable red sandstone battlements and massive polygonal towers enclose a vast compound. *Map F4 • 9am–6pm daily (to 8pm in summer) • Adm*

2 Castro Marim

The enormous frontier castle overlooks the border between Spain and Portugal. Built in the 13th century, the castle was the first headquarters of the Order of Christ. Henry the Navigator was a frequent visitor. *Map P3 • Apr–Oct: 9am–7pm daily; Nov–Mar: 9am–5pm • Free*

3 Alcoutim

Enjoying a lovely setting, Alcoutim commands glorious views across the River Guadiana and the Spanish town of Sanlúcar. Built in the 14th century, it was here that the short-lived peace treaty between Fernando I and Henrique of Castile was signed on 31 March, 1371. *Lago do Castelo • Map P1 • Adm*

4 Loulé

The immaculately restored battlements are an integral part of the town's historical make up. A wonderful little museum has been built into the castle walls which includes a recreation of a traditional Algarve kitchen. The view from the ramparts affords grand views. *Map J4 • 9am–5:30pm Mon–Fri, 10am–2pm Sat, closed Sun • Adm*

5 Tavira

Only the walls remain of this old Moorish fortification which surround a charming, well maintained garden. There are lovely views. *Map M4 • 8am–5pm Tue–Fri, 9am–5:30pm Sat, Sun and public hols, closed Mon • Free*

Alcoutim

6 Fortaleza de Sagres

The fortress is steeped in history and myth. Huge walls and bastions date from 1793: little, if anything, remains of Henry the Navigator's original fortress. Whether or not there was an academy of navigation founded here remains a matter of debate and legend. An 18th-century sun-dial fashioned into the wall is aligned with the famous wind compass *(see p28)*. *Map B6 • 10am–6pm daily (til 8.30pm May–Sep) • Adm*

Aljezur

7 Aljezur

Dominating the landscape around Aljezur are the ruins of the town's 10th-century castle. Perched on a hillock with fabulous views of the coast and Serra de Monchique, this Moorish stronghold controlled an ancient river port and provided a vital link with the open sea. Its broad, overgrown courtyard hides remnants of a vaulted cistern and is surrounded by high ramparts reinforced by two towers, one round, the other square. *Map C3 • Free*

8 Paderne

The atmospheric ruins of Paderne's long-abandoned Moorish castle are best appreciated on a Sunday morning when there's little traffic on the nearby motorway. The thick outer walls of mud and sandstone and the remains of a barbican tower are all that exist of the original structure. Inside, the chapel of Nossa Senhora da Assunção lies in mournful pieces. *Map G4 • Free*

9 Fortaleza Cacelha Velha

This pocket-sized fortress sits in the quaint hamlet of Cacelha Velha, 8 km (5 miles) west of Monte Gordo, in the eastern Algarve. Polygonal in shape, the building dates from the 18th century and overlooks a gentle lagoon teeming with waterfowl. Its squat turrets are topped with whitewashed cones. *Map N4 • Closed to public*

10 Salir

The ruins of Salir's Moorish castle have been put to novel effect by locals who have sunk gardens in between the battle-ments and the keep. The rest of the structure can be explored by treading a circular path around the middle of the fortifications. A small museum is under construction. *Map J3 • Free*

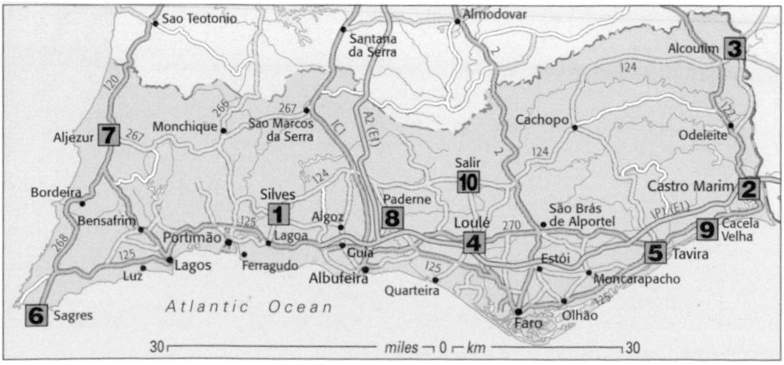

Left **Colourful livery on the Bom Dia** Centre **Riosul Guadiana** Right **Arade Mar river boat**

TOP 10 Coastal and River Cruises

Schooner Condor de Vilamoura

1 Condor de Vilamoura

Choose either a three-hour trip to Albufeira's coastal grottoes or a 7-hour cruise with beach barbecue at Armação de Pêra. *Cais I, 25, Marina de Vilamoura • Map H5 • (289) 312 941 • Mid-Mar–Nov*

2 Caravela Santa Bernarda

This replica of a 500-year-old Portuguese caravela charts the mysterious caves and grottoes between Lagos and Armação de Pêra. *Moored at Portimão quay • Map E4 • (282) 969 020 • Feb–Nov*

3 Bom Dia

This colourful schooner sets sail for the Ponte de Piedade grottoes, where dinghies allow closer inspection of this natural wonder. The all-day cruise sails on to Sagres and the "end of the world". *Marina de Lagos, 10 • Map D5 • (282) 764 670 • Mid-March–mid-Nov*

4 Dolphin Seafaris

Claiming an 80 percent success rate, this semi-inflatable powers out of the marina on its quest. When the dolphins are sighted, the boat reduces speed and waits for a display of marine antics. *Seafari Café, Marina de Lagos • Map D5 • (282) 792 586 • Apr–Nov*

5 Riosul Guadiana

A trip upstream along the slumbering Guadiana, passing the Reserva Natural do Sapal. Lunch at Foz de Odeleite and music and wine on the return leg. *Rua Tristão Vaz Teixeira, 15, Monte Gordo • Map P4 • (281) 510 201 • Apr–Nov*

6 Arade Mar

This ancient waterway allows for an absorbing journey

Left **Caravela Santa Bernarda** Right **Schooner Bom Dia**

Arade Mar cruise

to Silves *(see pp14–15)*, where you can explore for an hour before the return. ✆ *Rua Serpa Pinto, 19, Portimão • Map E4 • (965) 140 400*

7 Ilha Deserta Cruise

A maritime expedition through the myriad waterways of the Parque Natural da Ria Formosa, allowing possibly the best way to explore this diverse wetland. Lunch is at O Estaminé, which specializes in seafood. ✆ *Ilha Deserta Animaris • Map L6 • (289) 824 739*

8 Isaura

Under full sail, this majestic yacht hugs the coastline from Lagos to Cabo de Sâo Vicente *(see p91)*. The ship drops anchor for lunch near a sandy beach, with plenty of time for swimming. ✆ *Pontoon C, Marina de Lagos • Map D5 • (962) 783 760*

9 Trésor Champagne Cruises

If luxury is what you crave at sea, why not begin the voyage with champagne and canapés? And, if your cruise is more than four hours long, proceed with a salmon-and-caviar lunch. ✆ *Marina de Lagos • Map D5 • (965) 656 675*

10 Vila Vita Private Cruise

For the ultimate in style and sophistication, charter a private motor yacht, care of the Vila Vita Parc resort *(see p122)*. The last word in maritime luxury. ✆ *Vila Vita Parc, Armação de Pêra • Map F5 • (282) 315 310*

Top Ten Algarve Sporting Activities

1 Surfing

Surfers from around the world converge on the west coast beaches, notably Praia do Armado and Praia da Arrifana.

2 Windsurfing

The Atlantic westerlies, especially at Praia de Salema and Praia do Matinhal, are a treat for windsurfers.

3 Horse Riding

Through the countryside or over a bracing coastal path, riding a Lusitano horse is a joyful way to explore the land.

4 Game Fishing

Fishing expeditions depart from resorts and marinas throughout the summer in search of marlin and shark.

5 Scuba Diving

Sea caves, historic wrecks and a wealth of marine life await those who don wetsuit and aqualung and plunge into the Algarve depths.

6 Walking and Hiking

Guided walking tours take in rolling hills, mountain gullies and exhilarating coastal ranges.

7 Tennis

The Algarve's many tennis academies provide ample opportunity to better your game.

8 Sailing

The warm waters off the Algarve provide a natural arena for all type of sailing craft, from dinghy to schooner.

9 Cycling

Cycles can be hired by the hour by those who wish to explore at their own pace and off the beaten track.

10 Bullfighting

The Portuguese bullfighter, or *cavaleiro*, is on horseback, and the fight combines bravado with virtuoso horsemanship.

Left **Krazy World** Centre **Karting** Right **Zoomarine**

Top 10 Children's Attractions

1 Zoomarine

A superb theme park – part zoo, part funfair – all about the ocean. Sleek sharks, shoals of colourful tropical fish, turtles, crocodiles and marine birds are on the welcoming committee. Spectacular water shows featuring high-spirited dolphins, crafty sea lions and cheeky seals are other highlights. *Estrada Nacional 125, Guia, Albufeira • Map G5 • Jun–mid Sep: 10am–7:30pm daily • Adm*

2 Aqualand – The Big One

Head first or feet first, dare to disappear down one of the huge tubular water chutes and you will find yourself twisting and turning in spiralling loops to be discharged with a huge splash into a vast swimming pool below. This is Europe's biggest open-air waterpark and is set in a landscape of shady palms and trim gardens with lots to do between getting dunked. *Estrada Nacional 125, Alcantarilha • Map F4 • 10am–6:30pm • Adm*

Lagos Zoological Park

3 Krazy World

Snake pits, an alligator swamp, turtle town and iguana city feature at this highly unusual and wholly entertaining animal park. The pet farm is sanctuary to smaller, more cuddly creatures, while dinosaurs loom over the 18-hole crazy golf course that cuts a path through the jungles of the Lost World. *Estrada de Messines, Guia, Algoz • Map G5 • 9:30am–6pm daily (to 7:30pm in summer) • Closed in Jan • Adm*

4 A Cova dos Mouros

A unique theme park centred on a real prehistoric copper mine. Walk past echoing mine shafts and a marvellous reconstruction of a Neolithic village and hilltop fort. Donkey rides and swimming in a river are other activities. *Reserva da Foupana, Vaqueiros/Martin Longo • Map L1 • 10:30am–4:30pm daily; to 6pm in summer • Closed in bad weather • Adm*

5 Lagos Zoological Park

A menagerie of exotic and appealing wildlife. Bushy-tailed lemurs, sure-footed gibbons and rotund Vietnamese pigs share the grounds with graceful flamingos, leggy emus, beady-eyed toucans and wallabies who bounce around with abandon. *Sítio do Medronhal, Lagos • Map D5 • 10am–5pm daily (to 7pm in summer) • Adm*

6 Karting

Experience life in the fast lane at this challenging circuit, inaugurated by Ayrton Senna, with its exact replica of the famous Jacarepágua Formula 1 track in Brazil. A smaller circuit with less powerful machines is geared towards youngsters. *Vale d'Éguas, Almansil • Map J5 • 10am–7pm daily (to 8pm weekends) • Adm*

Slide & Splash

7 Roma Mini-Golf Park

A hole-in-one under the columns of a Roman temple? It's possible at this mini-golf park where life-sized replicas of villas, arcades and an amphitheatre reflect the Roman theme designed around the layout. *Avenida Cerro da Vila, Vilamoura • Map H5 • 10am–midnight daily (Mar–Nov)*

8 Slide & Splash

Corkscrew, Black Hole and Crazy River are some of the mesmerizing water chutes. The adrenaline rush starts working overtime when you're halfway down the Kamikaze water slide. *Parque de Divertimentos Aquáticos, Estrada 125, Vale de Deus, Estômbar, Lagoa • Map E4 • 10am–5:30pm daily (to 6:30pm in summer) • Adm*

9 Fábrica do Inglês

In summer this lively show ground is animated by clowns, dancers, jesters and musicians. Dazzling cybernetic water fountains play all day. As evening falls the fountains are the stage for the stunning multimedia "Aquavision" water show. *Rua Gregório Mascarenhas, Silves • Map F4 • 9am–midnight daily*

10 Zebra Safari

Discover the Algarve off road in a 4 x 4 jeep. Meet traditional handicraft artists and observe beekeepers collecting honey. There are also swimming opportunities and chances to sample local cuisine in this convivial activity park. *Agência de Viagens, Apartado 836, Arcadas de São João, Albufeira • Map G5 • 289 583 300 • 9am–6pm daily (summer)*

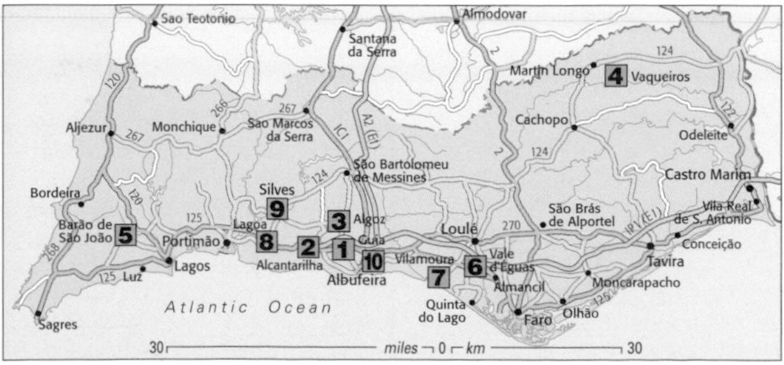

Left **Fatacil, Lagoa** Centre **Carnaval costumes, Loulé** Right **National Folklore Festival, Alte**

TOP 10 Festivals

1 Fatacil, Lagoa

The premier showcase for all things Algarve, this nine-day jamboree attracts visitors from all over Portugal. It is part agricultural show, part handicrafts fair – with a music concert, trade exhibition and gastronomy festival thrown in for good measure. *Fatacil showground, EN 125, Lagoa • Map E4 • Mid-Aug • Adm*

2 Carnival, Loulé

Carnival in Loulé is one of the biggest, brightest and boldest street parties in Portugal, a three-day extravaganza of mirth, mischief and merry-making. The procession of floats heaves with a colourful theatre of costumes, masks and hats. Festivities continue into the night with dancing till dawn. *Loulé town centre • Map J4 • Before Easter*

3 Medieval Fair, Castro Marim

Towards the end of the summer the town of Castro Marim returns to the Middle Ages to host a spectacular pageant in the grounds of the 13th-century castle. Archers draw their bows on mocking bullseye targets while mounted knights tilt their lances and jesters cajole the crowd with music and banter. At night, actors in period costume recreate medieval plays to a hushed audience. *Castro Marim • Map P3 • 31 Aug–2 Sep • Adm*

Folk musician

4 Algarve International Music Festival

Prestigious arts festival whose luminaries have included Luciano Pavarotti. A series of music, song and dance performances takes place mid-summer across the Algarve. It ranges from jazz to graceful ballet and from choral ensembles to melancholic *fado* (a kind of Portuguese blues). There's a thriving fringe element to the proceedings that is often ethnic in flavour and wonderfully surprising in nature. *Various regional venues • June and July • Adm*

5 National Folklore Festival

The entire Algarve becomes an impromptu stage as lively troupes of dancers and singer-musicians from across Portugal descend on the region for two weeks of spirited performances. It is a celebration of centuries-old culture, an insight into the charming and diverse world that is Portugal's folklore heritage. *Various regional venues • Mid-Sep*

6 Mãe Soberana, Loulé

This is the Algarve's most important religious festival, linked to ancient maternity rites. On Easter Sunday, a 16th-century statue of Mãe Soberana (the Sovereign Mother) is carried into town from her hilltop shrine. Exuding solemnity and piety, the subdued procession makes its way to Loulé's parish church where the image rests for two weeks. On the return journey the mood is more ebullient – flowers are tossed into the path of the cortège, and the air rings with cries of "Viva Mãe Soberana". *Loulé town centre • Map J4*

Mãe Soberana, Loulé

7 Silves Beer Festival

A few years ago the boisterous beer-fest was held within the grounds of the town's castle – an ironic fate to befall a former Muslim stronghold. Today, the ten-day drinking spree takes place in the far more conducive surrounds of the Fábrica do Inglês showground. *Silves • Map F4 • 29 Jun–8 Jul • Adm*

8 City Festival, Tavira

Every town in Portugal celebrates a municipal holiday. Tavira's celebrations are particularly vibrant, with a riot of colourful paper flowers and evergreen myrtle. Sardines sizzle on ad hoc braziers. The dancing and revelry continue well into the night. *Tavira town centre • Map M4 • 24–25 Jun*

9 Festival of the Smoked Sausage, Querença

A curious mix of pagan ritual and religious celebration. An auction of smoked sausage donated by residents takes place in homage to São Luís, the patron saint of animals, with the proceeds donated to charity. A modest cultural fair takes place at the same time, and visitors can sample hearty rural gastronomy. *Largo do Igreja, Querença • Map K4 • 20 Jan*

10 Seafood Festival, Olhão

Olhão is the Algarve's biggest fishing port, and at festival time numerous stalls groan under the weight of every imaginable seafood delicacy, including octopus, squid, clam, prawn, mussel and the ubiquitous grilled sardine. Folk music and dancing add further flavour. *Jardim Patrão Joaquim Lopes, Olhão • Map L5 • 10–15 Aug*

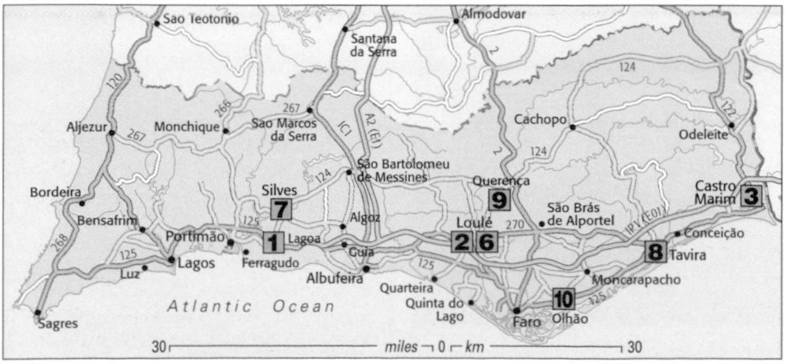

Left **Quinta Shopping** Right **Loulé market**

TOP 10 Shopping Malls and Markets

1 Forum Algarve, Faro

Created with much more than shopping in mind, Forum Algarve is the biggest mall of its kind in the region, attracting visitors and residents alike. Over 200 shops, boutiques and department stores, as well as an enormous hypermarket and family entertainment centre are imaginatively incorporated into an architectural design inspired by Faro's historic city centre. *Forum Algarve, EN 125, Faro • Map K6 • 9am–10pm daily*

2 Algarve Shopping, Guia

The exterior of this new shopping complex is striking in its colour scheme, following the geometric pattern of traditional Algarve architecture. The mall boasts more than 130 stores, 45 fashion boutiques, a hypermarket and food hall. *EN 125, Guia • Map G4 • 9am–10pm daily*

Algarve Shopping, Guia

3 Quinta Shopping, Quinta do Lago

The elegant mall with its open-air terraces and wide esplanades is situated within the exclusive Quinta do Lago estate. Well-known fashion houses showcase their latest ready-to-wear designs. Top-range jewellery, cosmetic and perfume stockists also have a presence. *Quinta do Lago, Almansil • Map J5 • 9am–10pm daily*

4 Loulé Market

On Saturday mornings this market bursts with the freshest harvest from the ocean and the hinterland. Delicate sprigs of herbs and spices hang over pots of honey and jam. Cakes made from fig and almond compete for space with loops of smoked sausage, fresh fish glisten and everywhere it seems are blooms of bright flowers. *Praça da República, Loulé • Map J4 • 9am–2pm Sat*

5 Centro Comercial de Portimão

Modest in size when compared with other malls in the region, Portimão nevertheless tempts shoppers with a choice of 62 stores selling everything from microwaves to shoe horns, bikinis to mountain bikes. *Quinta da Malata, Lote 1, Portimão • Map E4 • 9am–10pm daily; Hypermarket closed Sun*

6 Apolónia Supermarket, Almansil

Shoppers in the know travel here from right across the length and breadth of the region. Foreign produce such as fresh Argentinean beef, macaroni pasta and spicy tandoori curry powder feature. The cosmopolitan wine selection includes bottles from California, Chile and Australia. *271 Avenida 5 de Outubro, Almansil • Map J5 • 8am–8pm Mon–Sat, 9am–1pm Sun*

7 Quarteira Fish Market

Easily the best-loved fish market in the region, straight off the boat. Animated bartering takes place at dawn on the quayside. The throng is usually greatest around the famous Quarteira prawns. *Largo do Peixe, Quarteira • Map H5 • 9am–1pm Wed*

8 Rua da Barbaca, Loulé

If one thoroughfare deserves the epithet "artisan's street", it's this unassuming road near Loulé Castle. The artists tout mini works of art in copper, leather, wood and iron. The handicrafts are as authentic as you'll ever get and superb value for money. *Rua da Barbaca, Loulé • Map J4*

9 Olaria Algarve Porches Pottery

The blue and white façade of the building is unmistakable, and the pottery produced here is equally striking. Rows of women gossip merrily amongst themselves while deftly applying a final lick of paint to the latest batch of crockery. *EN 125, Porches, Lagoa • Map E4 • 9am–6pm Mon–Fri, 10am–2pm Sat*

Forum Algarve, Faro

10 Olhão Market

Situated right on the esplanade overlooking the lagoons, this is a fantastic place to shop for fresh fish, fruit and vegetables and flowers. A riot of noise and colour takes place daily under two purpose-built pavilions. On Saturdays it is enlivened by extra stalls selling anything from basketware and smoked sausage to honey and lace. *Avenida 5 de Outubro, Olhão • Map L5 • 7am–2pm Tue–Fri, 6:30am–3pm Sat*

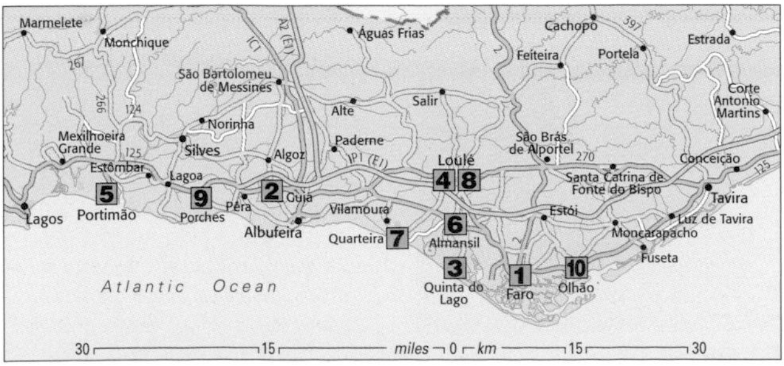

Left **Bar Bubi, Tavira** Centre **"The Strip", Albufeira** Right **Stevie Ray's Blues Jazz Bar, Lagos**

Top 10 Clubs and Late-Night Bars

1 Kiss, Albufeira

Arguably the most famous of all the Algarve nightclubs, Kiss is the talk of the town for its memorable party nights and zany theme festivals. Three dance floors reverberate to cutting-edge house, techno and hip-hop, attracting seasoned clubbers from all over the continent. Kiss starts to smoulder around 3am and is still sizzling at dawn. *Areias de São João, Albufeira • Map G5*

2 Kadoc, Vilamoura

A sprawling venue of gargantuan proportions, the nightclub can accommodate up to 7,000 party-goers on five dance floors illuminated by a spectacular tricolour laser system. The clientele is young and energetic. A landscaped open-air terrace set in a tropical garden offers a great spot for those chill-out sessions. It's always the last club to wind down, closing around 7am. *Estrada de Vilmoura • Map H5 • From midnight Sat, Sun, Mon • "Kadoc Club" from midnight Fri, Sat, Sun, Mon*

Kiss, Albufeira

3 Bar Capicua, Portimão

While neigbouring Praia da Rocha remains one of the Algarve's hottest nightclub districts, the town's nearby marina boasts some wonderful new bars including this one. The first-floor terrace is perfect on those balmy summer evenings when you'd rather chat quietly over a drink than join the throng on the dance floor where the music matches the mood – hot! *Marina de Portimão, Bloco 4, Portimão • Map E4 • 3pm–4am daily in summer*

4 Liberto's, Albufeira

One of the must-see nightclubs, rivalling Kiss in popularity. Football stars and TV personalities number among its summertime clientele. The esplanade (a favourite location for fashion shows) is replete with swimming pool and palm trees. Inside, a giant screen relays 24-hour cable TV broadcasts. By midnight, however, the DJ takes centre stage and the speakers positively shudder with sound. *Areias de São João, Albufeira • Map G5*

5 T-Club, Quinta do Lago

This is where the jet set congregates over the summer months for cocktails and exotic Japanese cuisine. The venue is an exercise in design elegance, with the patio built around verdant tropical gardens featuring water cascades. The prices are equally discerning. *Buganvilla Plaza, Quinta do Lago, Almansil • Map J5*

6 Round Up Saloon, Carvoeiro

With a bronco-bucking atmosphere, the Round Up looks and feels like a Texas saloon. "Outlaws" are locked up in a jail on the whim of Big Will the bartender and freed only on the promise of a beer. Live rock music is on most nights, and budding musicians are encouraged to jam. At weekends the karaoke cavalry arrives. *1 Estrada do Farol, Praia do Carvoeiro • Map E5 • 8pm–2am daily*

7 Discoteca Ubi and Bar Bubi, Tavira

Clubbers who pile out of Discoteca Ubi at 6am on a Sunday morning swear it's the best time they've had in their lives. It's not just the heavy house and trip-hop that packs them in. Ubi also stages some great theme nights, including wild foam parties. *Antiga Fábrica Balsense, Rua Almirante, Cândido dos Reis, Tavira • Map M4*

8 Stevie Ray's Blues Jazz Bar, Lagos

Toe-tapping live jazz on Saturday nights lifts this already excellent late-night bar to new heights. The atmosphere is pure Dixie, with the music varying from rocking blues to mellow swing. Smart/casual dress code. *9 Rua Srº da Graça, Lagos • Map D5 • 8:30pm–2am Tue–Sat*

Katedral, Praia da Rocha

9 Phoenix, Lagos

Unmistakable with its white-washed façade emblazoned with black and red livery, the venue is a huge hit with locals and visitors alike who pack the dance floor and grind to a musical mêlée of house, soul and ethnic rhythm. *Travessa do Cotovello, Lagos • Map D5*

10 Katedral, Praia da Rocha

Bright red neon announces this temple of sound, dedicated to playing whatever's current. Its three bars flank a central dance floor that's never big enough to accommodate the throngs of party people. A sprawling terrace bar at the back affords great views of the beach and is an ideal chill-out spot, fanned by sea breezes. *Avenida Tomás Cabreira, Praia da Rocha, Portimão • Map E5*

Left **Bifes de Atum** Right **Vineyard in the Algarve**

Top 10 Culinary Highlights of the Algarve

1 Ameijoas na Cataplana

If there is one dish synonymous with the Algarve's rich ocean harvest, it's this one. Fresh cockles are sealed in a *cataplana*, a rounded copper cooking vessel resembling a wok. Allowed to cook in their own steam with a combination of *presunto* (cured ham), *chouriço* (sausage), tomato, lemon, olive oil and garnished with coriander and garlic, the result is a succulent seafood delight. Enjoy with chilled white wine.

Porco à alentejana

Sardines assadas

2 Arroz de Polvo

A regional speciality which again evokes the Algarve's love affair with the sea. Tender morsels of fresh octopus are added to a mix of fried onion and parsley, and then gently boiled with wine vinegar and a dash of chilli powder. Rice is added with salt and pepper to taste. The meal is usually served with a side dish of black olives and generous slices of crusty bread.

Cabrito assado

3 Sardines Assadas

The humble and ubiquitous sardine is arguably the most popular menu choice in the region. Bursting with goodness, sardines are at their plumpest during summer, and are simply mouth-watering when charcoal grilled and served with boiled potatoes and salad.

4 Bifes de Atum

The livelihoods of whole communities used to depend on tuna. It's not fished so hard now, but is still a favourite in thousands of restaurants along the coast. Try *atum de cebola*, a tasty blend of melted butter and tomato sauce with onions, garlic and parsley, poured over a firm tuna steak garnished with lemon wedges.

5 Cabrito Assado

Roasted kid is what country folk sit down to. The meat is brushed with a thin layer of lard to keep it moist, sprinkled with minced bacon and laced with white wine. Garnished with whole garlic cloves and dusted liberally with paprika, it's then slowly roasted until crispy brown. Rich and wholesome, this truly is one of the great gastronomic wonders of rural Algarve.

6 Porco à Alentejana

This intrepid marriage of pork and clams appears to bring the ocean and the countryside together, although it's a feast

Doces de amêndoa

that originated in the vast plains of the Alentejo. The ingredients are cooked in a spicy marinade of white wine, fresh garlic and paprika. If prepared correctly, the shells should be open when served.

7 Frango Assado com Piri-piri

The great Portuguese stand-by: some restaurants in the Algarve serve nothing else. Generous platters of juicy chicken portions are served with crisp french fries and green-pepper salad. The meat comes dabbed with red chilli sauce, which is home-made and usually hot.

8 Gaspacho do Algarve

This version of gaspacho soup differs from its well-known Spanish counterpart in that the ingredients are not pulverized and so it retains a delightfully crunchy texture. Served cold, this heavenly blend of tomato, garlic, cucumber, oregano and sweet pepper sprinkled with diced crouton is bliss on a hot day.

9 Morgado de Figo

Figs were introduced by the Moors and soon became an integral part of Algarve cuisine. Fig lord cakes are dainty creations moulded from a fig-and-almond paste.

10 Doces de Amêndoa

Almonds (another Moorish import) are used to make these colourful little delicacies that can look like fish, fruit, birds, smiling faces and even vegetable baskets. They make wonderful coffee companions or little gifts.

Top 10 Wines, Liqueurs and Spirits

1 Vila Santa

A full-bodied Alentejo red made from a blend of grapes trodden by foot in marble vats.

2 Herdade Grande Colheita Selecionada

A delicious white from the Alentejo with a full, rich palate, creamy texture and soft finish. Ideal with baked fish, salad or chicken dishes.

3 Espirito

Distilled from the *moscatel* grape, this unique brandy has a strong kick and mildly sweet aftertaste.

4 Medronho

The celebrated *aguardiente* (brandy) is produced commercially, but the best is the "Monchique Moonshine", which is distilled in secret and sold with a nod and a wink.

5 Amarguinha

A sweet bitter-almond liqueur from the Algarve, ideal as an apéritif or digestif.

6 Vinha D'Ervideira

A young sparkling wine from the northern reaches of the Alentejo.

7 Aperitivo Seco Algarseio

Underrated Algarvian dry white apéritif wine which is similar to an amontillado.

8 Licor de Tangerina

Wonderfully fragrant liqueur with the tang of lush citrus groves.

9 Brandy-mel

A potent mix of brandy and honey, this is a favourite mid-winter tipple.

10 Bagaceira

Distilled from grape residue, this no-nonsense brandy is good for chasing down a strong black coffee.

For more on Alentejan wines See p108

Left **Quatro Águas, Tavira** Centre **Oasis, Carvoeiro** Right **Barroca, Lagos**

Top 10 Restaurants

1 Vila Joya, Albufeira

An exclusive gourmet restaurant boasting two Michelin stars. The menu degustation errs towards French haute cuisine, with a superb wine list to match. The terrace has a magnificent sea view. Tables are strictly by reservation only, and the dress code is on the casual side of smart. *Praia da Galé, Apartado 120, Albufeira • Map G5 • (289) 591 839 • Closed 11 Nov–2 Mar • €€€€€*

Chef, Vila Joya

2 Henrique Leis, Almansil

A Michelin star shines above this Swiss chalet-style restaurant where creativity and innovation are the hallmarks of the menu. Intimate surrounds are enhanced by colourful artwork adorning the walls. Smart to casual dress. *Vale Formoso, Almansil • Map J5 • (289) 393 438 • Closed Thu • No vegetarian dishes • €€€€*

3 Adega Vilalisa, Mexilhoeira Grande

Renowned Portuguese food critic José Quitério regards this charming rural eatery as one of the best 100 restaurants in the country. Sample traditional dishes such as the *canja de conquilhas* (cockle broth) and you'll understand why. Book in advance. *52 Rua Francisco Bivar, Mexilhoeira Grande • Map D4 • (282) 968 478 • No vegetarian dishes • €*

Henrique Leis, Almansil

4 Casa Velha, Quinta do Lago

French haute cuisine is served in this 300-year-old converted farmhouse. It will appeal to the seasoned gourmet as well as the wine connoisseur: there are over 200 Portuguese reds alone to choose from! *Quinta do Lago, Almansil • Map J5 • (289) 394 983 • No credit cards • No vegetarian dishes • €€€*

5 Quatro Águas, Tavira

A restaurant famed for its views over the lagoon as much for its wonderful *camarão vermelho flamejado* (flaming red shrimp) and *borrego com estragão* (lamb seasoned with tarragon). *Quatro Águas, Tavira • Map M4 • (281) 325 329 • Closed Mon • €*

6 O Charneco, Estômbar

Larger-than-life proprietor Joaquim Charneco and his wife Marta have scooped numerous culinary awards for their delicious choice of rustic fare. Traditional wood-burning ovens give the food its distinct flavour. *3 Rua D.Sancho II, Estômbar • Map E4 • (282) 431 113 • €*

For restaurant price bands **See p81**

Barroca, Lagos

7 Sueste, Ferragudo

The bizarre-looking but incredibly tasty *emparador* (emperor fish) is one of the more unusual treats on the menu at this fabulous quayside restaurant overlooking the River Arade. Spectacular summer sunsets bathe the terrace with a golden light, adding greatly to Sueste's appeal.
Rua da Ribeira 91, Ferragudo • Map E5 • (282) 461 592 • No credit cards • No vegetarian dishes • €

8 Oasis, Carvoeiro

This cosy Dutch-run restaurant exudes a personality all of its own. Generous portions are served in candlelit surrounds, or out on a patio that fills rapidly on summer evenings. Highly recommended is the *entrecosto estilo Americano* (spare ribs American style).
34 Rua do Barranco, Praia do Carvoeiro • Map E5 • (282) 357 332 • No credit cards • Closed Sun • €

9 Barroca, Lagos

Vivid Mexican creations such as *camarões grelhados* (grilled prawns tossed in tabasco and coriander) spice up the menu in the same colourful manner as the interior decoration of this energetic Latino-European eatery. *1 Rua da Barroca, Lagos • Map D5 • (282) 767 162 • No Credit Cards • €*

10 Mesa dos Mouras, Faro

Faro's historic 13th-century cathedral overlooks this quiet, rustic establishment, the name of which translates as "The Moors' Table". The *javoli com molho de frutos* (wild boar with fruit sauce) is a much loved classic from the restaurant's range of Southern Portuguese cuisine. *10 Largo da Sé, 8000 Faro • Map K6 • (289) 878 873 • No credit cards • No vegetarian dishes • €*

Mesa dos Mouras, Faro

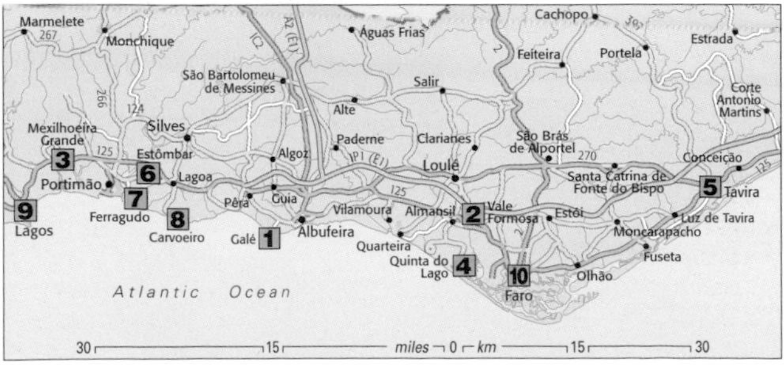

DOM MARCELINO
BISPO DO ALGARVE

AROUND THE ALGARVE

Left **Faro Marina** Centre **Carving, São Lourenço church, Almansil** Right **Church, Salir**

Central Region

THE ALGARVE'S CENTRAL REGION encompasses the busiest coastal resorts in southern Portugal as well as remote inland hamlets. It's an area of widely contrasting character, blessed with superb golf courses, beautiful golden beaches and wild, rolling hills where a more traditional, rural way of life prevails. History has left its indelible mark throughout this land in the shape of Stone Age megaliths, the remains of Roman villas, imposing Moorish castles and noble Gothic cathedrals. A strong, proud maritime heritage pervades the coast, evident in the fine selection of seafood in seaside restaurants.

Top 10 Sights

1. Faro
2. Silves
3. Loulé
4. Albufeira
5. Vilamoura
6. Almansil
7. Alte
8. Portimão
9. Salir
10. Ferragudo

Bishop's Palace, Faro

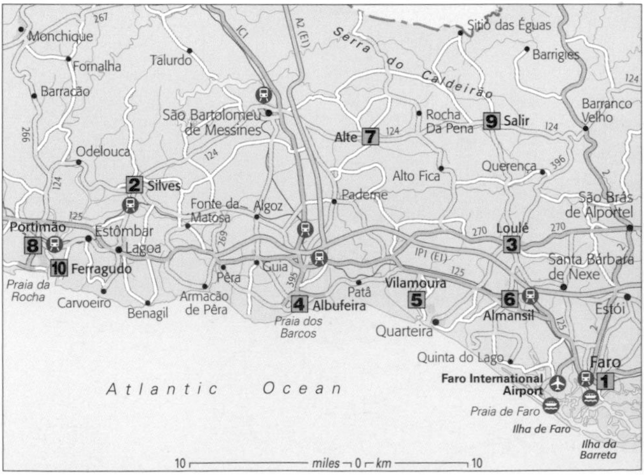

Previous pages **Quiet square in Tavira**

Saturday market, Loulé

1 Faro

Faro is often overlooked by visitors to the Algarve who tend to head straight for the beach resorts. This is unfortunate, because its Old Town quarter is a particularly enchanting ensemble of centuries-old architecture and fine museums worthy of thorough investigation. Of special merit is the former convent of Nossa Senhora da Assunção, which houses the city's excellent archaeological museum *(see pp8 & 44)*.

2 Silves

Overlooking a fertile valley of lemon and orange groves, cork and almond trees and swathes of scented meadows is Silves. Once the grandiose capital of Moorish Algarve, the town's main draw is its castle. As well as taking the inspiring walk around its red sandstone battlements, visitors should look out for the fabulous vaulted Moorish cistern and Traitor's gate – the battle-scarred doorway through which Dom Paio Peres Correira stormed to recapture the stronghold for Christian forces in 1242. Outside the castle walls is the 13th-century cathedral, which was the seat of the Algarve see until 1580 *(see pp14–15)*.

3 Loulé

This cheerful market town is renowned as a centre of traditional handicraft. The copper, leather and ceramic goods hammered out in the dozens of workshops dotted around its streets are some of the most sought-after in the Algarve. These can be purchased at Loulé's bustling Saturday morning market along with an amazing selection of fruit and vegetables, fresh fish, herbs, spices, honey, bottled liqueurs and sugared fig cakes. Loulé was an important Moorish settlement, and remnants of Muslim rule still exist *(see pp18–19)*.

4 Albufeira

Albufeira's claim as the most popular holiday destination in the country is no idle boast. It's the biggest and most energetic resort in the Algarve, and anyone doubting the fact should make a midsummer bee-line to the thoroughfare dubbed "The Strip". A forest of neon lends the resort its exotic, all-night atmosphere, and a multitude of bars, restaurants and disco-clubs keep the party swinging till dawn. You can catch up on sleep on any one of Albufeira's smooth, golden beaches, if you can find a spot amongst fellow sun-worshippers *(see pp30–31)*.

Silves

Left **Church, Almansil** Centre **Azulejos, Alte** Right **Praia de Rocha, Portimão**

5 Vilamoura

With its refined edge, glamorous reputation and celebrity status, Vilamoura is the resort choice for the well-heeled, where the yacht set and jet set rub shoulders. The boardwalk is also the jumping-off point for coastal cruises on graceful schooners, and shark and marlin fishing expeditions. The region as a whole is of great environmental and historical significance – the wetland surrounding the resort is a protected nature reserve, and the Cerro da Vila *(see p44)* is one of the most important Roman sites in Portugal. *Map H5*

6 Almansil

One of the most resplendent of all the Algarve's treasures is the 18th-century Igreja Matriz de São Lourenço, just outside the unexceptional village of Almansil. Outstanding *azulejos* panels in the church depict episodes in the life of St Lawrence, while the highly ornate cupola is a breathtaking exercise in trompe-l'oeil – some say the best example of its kind outside Rome. *Map J5*

7 Alte

Described as "a delightful snapshot of the real Algarve" in many a tourist brochure, Alte is indeed a picture of beauty and serenity. The little village with its whitewashed façades, filigree chimney pots and rural charm appears to have little time for the 21st century, but always greets visitors with a warm handshake and ready smile. The central attraction is the Igreja da Matriz. The area is also renowned for its handicrafts and colourful folklore. *Map H3*

The Carob Bean

Worth its weight in gold, the versatile carob bean tree is found in abundance throughout the Caldeirão mountain region. The beans are mainly used as animal feed but also as a chocolate substitute. Pods can be ground and mixed with wheat flour to produce tasty black bread. The gum is used in the textile and pharmaceutical industries.

8 Portimão

Portimão's principal draw is its wide, sweeping esplanade which makes for an effortless afternoon stroll. One detour worth taking, though, is to the garden in Largo 1° de Dezembro, which has a series of stone benches ornamented with 19th-century azulejos depicting historical events. Regular cruise boats head towards Silves or chart a more bracing course along the coast. The town's riverfront restaurants dish up generous helpings of succulent charcoal-grilled sardines. *Map E4*

9 Salir

In springtime, wild flowers of every hue blanket the meadows around this hilltop hamlet, with its ruined 12th-century Moorish castle. The terraced battlements are now reclaimed to ingenious effect by enterprising locals who use them as vegetable plots. The short walk around the castle foundations is rewarded with an inviting panorama over the limestone *massif* of Rocha da Pena. The area is a known nesting site for the huge eagle owl. Naturalists may also be lucky enough to spy the odd genet or Egyptian mongoose. *Map J3*

10 Ferragudo

Ferragudo has admirably managed to avoid the more garish trappings of tourism and looks the better for it. Sitting at the mouth of the Rio Arade, this attractive fishing village tumbles down to a busy little quayside bristling with fishermen's huts, artisan's workshops and one or two truly memorable seafood restaurants. The maze of steep cobbled alleys lead up to a rather handsome church. Praia Grande is a generous swathe of sand, which is popular sunbathing territory and also the location of a big windsurfing school. The beach is dominated by the monolithic Fortaleza de São João, a private residence. *Map E5*

Ferragudo

A Tour of Villages

Morning

An ideal starting point for your drive is **Loulé** *(p71)* on a Saturday morning to take advantage of the bustling market. An early start will ensure you get the best choice of the produce. Aim to get there about 9am and allow an hour for browsing the stalls.

Order a coffee in Café Calcinha, Praça da República, 67, before jumping in the car and heading west on the N270 to the village of **Paderne** *(p76)*. If you want to visit the 12th-century Moorish castle, turn right before the village.

To reach the next village, **Alte**, double back and head towards São Bartolomeu de Messines, turning right at the N124. Alte is now signposted, and you'll reach it within half an hour. Take time to explore this wonderful rural idyll.

Afternoon

Lunch should be savoured in **Salir**, a leisurely, 25-minute drive away. Try the Casa Pasto Mouro Bar, in Rua dos Muros do Castelo, below the castle ruins and with superb views of Rocha da Pena.

Continue east on the N124, driving through the Caldeirão mountain range before turning right onto the N396, back towards Loulé.

A signposted detour off this road will take you into the ancient hamlet of **Querença** *(p76)*, with its whitewashed church and the Loja da Quinta, a wonderful little handicrafts store. Treat yourself to some local liqueurs before heading back to Loulé.

Left **Carvoeiro** Centre **Querença** Right **Paderne**

Top 10 Other Villages and Sights

1 Paderne
A world away from the villas and beaches of the Algarve coast. The faded, timeworn charm is mirrored by some lovely 19th-century buildings. The half dozen friendly café-restaurants dotted around the vicinity make for welcome refreshment. *Map G4*

2 Querença
A quaint hamlet slumbering in isolated beauty and crowned by the simple Igreja Nossa Senhora da Assunção. *Map K4*

3 São Bartolomeu de Messines
Poet João de Deus (1830–96) is synonymous with this quiet rural town. The church has some amazing twisted sandstone pillars – unique in the Algarve. *Map G3*

4 Vaqueiros
This remote village is the site of a copper-goldmine worked by a Muslim labour force some 900 years ago, now an imaginative theme park. *Map M2*

5 Ameixial
Typical of the villages that pepper this rugged region. Nearby Miradoura de Caldeirão is an inspiring place for a picnic, and to the south are the last remaining examples of round dwellings. *Map K2*

6 Santa Catarina da Fonte do Bispo
The village is mainly famous for its traditional red clay bricks and roof tiles. Some of the local olive trees are believed to be more than 1,000 years old. *Map L4*

7 Giões
Rarely visited, and best in mid-summer when the area is awash with bright pink oleander, the village is known for its handmade bamboo baskets and rustic chairs. Nearby are the ruins of a fort and two mills. *Map M1*

8 Praia do Carvoeiro
Picturesque beach wedged between steep-sided cliffs and framed by rows of holiday apartments and some excellent restaurants. A popular summer haunt for families and, during the winter months, golfers. *Map E5*

9 Alcantarilha
Known for its gruesome bone chapel, with the skeletal remains of 1,500 former parishioners completely covering the ceilings and walls. *Map F4*

The bone chapel at Alcantarilha

10 Alcalar
The Alcalar burial chambers are a series of Neolithic dolmen passage tombs. The drive here is a delight in itself, among ancient oak and olive trees. *Map D4*

Previous pages **Beach at Albufeira**

Left **Praia de São Rafael, Albufeira** Centre **Praia de Faro** Right **Praia da Marinha, Benagil**

Top 10 Beaches

1 Praia do Barcos, Albufeira

The "Beach of Boats" is so called because of the dozens of colourful fishing smacks pulled up on the sand between use. *Map G5*

2 Praia de São Rafael, Albufeira

Some extraordinary rock formations protrude from the shallows of this pretty bay fringed with fine sand. *Map G5*

3 Praia da Oura, Albufeira

Located at the bottom of "The Strip", this is a hugely popular beach in summer and attractive with its patches of yellow sandstone rock. *Map G5*

4 Praia de Rocha, Portimão

One of the most famous beaches in the Algarve, this impressive swathe of golden sand stretches out in front of russet-coloured cliffs. *Map E4*

5 Praia de Marinha, Benagil

An almost vertical cliff face towers over Marinha's two wonderfully secluded beaches, the waters of which are a favourite with snorkellers. *Map F5*

6 Praia da Falésia, Olhos de Agua

A long, narrow beach that never gets too crowded in summer. It's exposed to fresh south-westerlies so draws the windsurfing set. A good option if peace and quiet are the order of the day. *Map H5*

7 Praia da Vilamoura

The beach at Vilamoura enjoys an enviable location right next to the resort. Its waters are calmed by the harbour breakwater, and the place is often used as a backdrop by fashion photographers. *Map H5*

8 Praia do Vale do Lobo

This select beachfront is patronized by guests staying at the nearby Vale do Lobo resort and is always a hive of activity. There are some excellent bar-cafés close at hand. *Map J5*

9 Praia de Faro (Ilha de Faro)

One of the narrow barrier islands that shelter the Ria Formosa lagoon, this giant sand spit is a magnet for Faro residents and those visitors wishing to escape the city heat mid-season. *Map J–K6*

Albufeira

10 Praia da Galé, Armação de Pêra

Two half-moons of smooth white sand make up this beach, interrupted by some weird outcrops of ochre-splashed sandstone. *Map F5*

Left **San Lorenzo Golf Club** Right **Balaia Golf**

Top 10 Golf Courses

1 San Lorenzo Golf Club
The magnificent, 18-hole, par 72 course is considered by *World Golf* magazine to be one of Europe's top five courses. *Almansil • Map J5 • (289) 396 534*

2 Quinta do Lago Golf Clubs
Quinta do Lago, a championship course, has hosted the Portuguese Open several times. It is especially notable for four excellent par 5 holes. *Almansil • Map J5 • (289) 390 700*

3 Sheraton Pine Cliffs
This 9-hole, par 33 clifftop course is set against a spectacular Atlantic Ocean backdrop. The last hole is named "Devil's Parlour". *Praia da Falésia, Albufeira • Map G5 • (289) 500 113*

4 Vale do Lobo Golf Resort
The Royal Course incorporates the world-famous par 3 16th hole with an extensive carry over cliffs. The Ocean Course follows an undulating layout. *Almansil • Map J5 • (289) 353 535*

5 Vilamoura Golf Course
The Old Course, Pinhal, Laguna and Millennium courses are all fabulous 18-hole, par 72 layouts, in a beautiful natural setting with pinewood and lake. *Lusotur Golfes, Vilamoura • Map H5 • (289) 310 333*

6 Penina Golf
The masterpiece 18-hole, par 73 Championship course was designed by golf guru Sir Henry Cotton and has hosted the Portuguese Open. *Estrada Nacional 125, Portimão • Map E4 • (282) 420 200*

7 Pestana Hotels & Resorts Carvoeiro
An ancient olive tree spreads over one of the greens of the 18-hole Pinta course. The 18-hole Gramacho layout has some heavily bunkered greens. *Map E5 • (282) 340 900*

8 Pinheiros Altos
An independent 18-hole, par 72 course built on the Quinta do Lago estate, embracing part of the Parque Natural da Ria Formosa. *Q. do Lago • Map J5 • (289) 359 910*

9 Vila Sol Golf
Known for its water hazards, this 27-hole, par 72 course is a suitable challenge for golfers of all handicap levels. *Alto do Semino, Estrada Nacional 396, Vilamoura • Map H5 • (289) 300 505*

10 Balaia Golf
Built on pleasant undulating terrain punctuated with umbrella pine, cork oak and carob trees, this executive 9-hole, par 27 course opened in 2001. *Albufeira • Map G5 • (289) 570 442*

Pinheiros Altos Golf Club

Left **Loulé market** Centre **Olaria Algarve pottery** Right **Quarteira fish market**

Top 10 Places to Shop

1 Loulé Market

One of the Algarve's biggest and most colourful markets, selling fruit and vegetables, fish, herbs, spices, honey, jams, cakes and local handicraft. ⊛ *Praça da República, Loulé • Map J4 • 9am–2pm Sat*

Loulé market

2 Forum Algarve Shopping Centre

With an architectural design inspired by Faro's historical centre, this is the region's biggest shopping mall. ⊛ *EN 125, Sítio das Figuras, Faro • Map K6*

3 Algarve Shopping Centre

Modern mall with national and international chains, hypermarket, multi-screen cinema and food hall. ⊛ *EN 125, Guia • Map G4*

4 Quinta Shopping Centre

An elegant open-air mall with some designer boutiques beauty salons, sports outlets and several restaurants. ⊛ *Quinta do Lago • Map J5*

5 Centro Comercial Modelo de Portimão

The Modelo hypermarket is the huge anchor store in this busy shopping complex. ⊛ *Quinta da Malata, Lote 1, Portimão • Map E4*

6 Apolónia Supermarket

The best supermarket in the land for imported foreign produce difficult to get elsewhere in Portugal. ⊛ *Avenida 5 de Outubro, 271, Almansil • Map J5*

7 Porches Pottery

One of the first commercial ceramic outlets in the region. The vast array of glazed pottery and earthenware goods are all manufactured in-house. Superb value for money. ⊛ *EN 125, Porches, Lagoa • Map E4*

8 Loja da Quinta

With its impressive range of home-made liqueurs and opportunities to sample some delicious regional fare, this modest handicrafts store in Querença's main square is definitely worth the drive. ⊛ *Lago da Igreja, Querença • Map K4*

9 Quarteira Fish Market

The most famous market of its kind on the south coast; arrive early for the choicest fish and seafood. Superb value for money makes this popular with restaurateurs as well as the public. ⊛ *Largo do Peixe, Quarteira • Map H5 • 9am–1pm Wed*

10 Planet Golf

The biggest chain in Portugal selling golf equipment and sport fashion. Staff are knowledgeable about the game. ⊛ *Avenida 5 de Outubro, 362 Apartado, Faro • Map K6*

Left **Kiss, Albufeira** Right **Katedral, Praia da Rocha**

TOP 10 Nightlife

1 Kiss, Albufeira

Possibly the best-known nightclub in Portugal. Attracting a mixed 20-something crowd, its resident and guest DJs spin a funky mix of house and hip-hop *(see p62)*.

2 Vilamoura Marina

A multitude of bars, eateries and late-night shopping. Spectacular firework displays round off many a long summer evening. *Map H5*

3 Vilamoura Casino

Sophisticated gaming room with baccarat, Portuguese dice, roulette (French and American), blackjack and 500 big-jackpot slot machines. The Mira Lago Room stages world-class music and dance. *Praça do Casino, Vilamoura • Map H5 • 7pm–3am daily*

Vilamoura Casino

4 Kadoc, Vilamoura

The biggest club in the Algarve draws thousands of revellers to its wild summer parties. Guests bump and grind on five tiered dance floors under a blaze of multicoloured light *(see p62)*.

5 Avenida Tomás Cabreira, Praia da Rocha

One of the first tourist resorts in the Algarve, with a long esplanade crammed with glitzy bars and trendy nightclubs. *Map E5*

6 Hotel Algarve Casino, Praia da Rocha

The first hotel-casino in Portugal is situated in a prime position. There's a fabulous slot machines room with 322 of the latest game stations. *Avenida Tomás Cabreira • Map E5 • 4pm–4am daily*

7 Katedral, Praia da Rocha

Popular late-night dance venue and a hit with young business professionals as well as the tuned-in youth. The sounds played out reflect whatever's current, but with the base level permanently off the dial *(see p63)*.

8 Pátio Disco Bar, Quinta do Lago

Friendly atmosphere, and a sprawling patio. A young, fun-loving crowd. *Map J5 • 6ª Rotunda • 10:30pm–6am Sat, Sun; daily in Aug*

9 Melting Pot, Quinta do Lago

Jolly, English pub-style bar and restaurant heaving with jovial locals, seasoned expatriates and sunburnt tourists. *Lote 27 Quinta Shopping • Map J5 • 10am–2pm daily*

10 Oficina Bar, Carvoeiro

A great late-night bar with a loyal following. *Oficina* means garage, relating to the décor, not the music. Cocktail shots must be downed in one! *Rua dos Pescadores, 75 • Map E5 • midnight–4am Mon–Sat*

Price Categories

For a three-course meal for one with half a bottle of wine (or equivalent meal), taxes and extra charges.

€	under €20
€€	€20–€30
€€€	€30–€40
€€€€	€40–€50
€€€€€	over €50

Left **Pasta Picasso, Loulé** Right **Casa Pasto Mouro Bar, Salir**

TOP 10 Restaurants

1 Ramires, Albufeira

Diners have been coming to this convivial restaurant since 1964 to sample the best chicken *piri-piri* in the Algarve. *Rua 25 de Abril, Guia • Map G5 • (289) 561 232 • €*

2 A Ruína, Albufeira

Seafood crams the chalked-up menu. The *Pargo* (sea bream) and *robalo* (sea bass) are particularly good. *Cais Herculano (Praia dos Barcos) • Map G5 • (289) 512 094 • €*

3 Pasta Picasso, Loulé

Intimate, candlelit interior suitably daubed with Cubist prints. The pasta is equally creative and appetising. *Rua Engº Duarte Pacheco, 116 • Map J4 • (289) 416 034 • €€*

4 Restaurante de Querença, Querença

The *ensopado de cabrito* (kid stew) is a house speciality at this wonderfully provincial restaurant, which overlooks Fonte Benémola and a lovely old church. *Largo da Igreja, Querença • Map J4 • (289) 422 540 • €*

5 Tarantino's, Quinta do Lago

Offering an intriguing fusion of Italian gastronomy and Asian specialities, the delicious East-meets-West menu is highly creative. Advance booking advisable. *Quinta Shopping • Map J5 • (289) 392 395 • €€€*

6 Casa Pasto Mouro Bar, Salir

Built on the ramparts of the Moorish castle. Wholesome fare is served by villagers, making this a rural experience to savour. Arrive early. *Map J3 • Rua dos Muros do Castelo • (289) 489 458 • €*

7 Marisqueira Rui, Silves

Order *ameijoas na cataplana* (cockles in a *cataplana* pan) and you'll understand why this is the most famous seafood restaurant in the Algarve. *Rua Comendador Vilarinho, 32 • Map F4 • (282) 442 682 • €*

8 Sueste, Ferragudo

Renowned for its fabulous range of seafood dishes, such as *pargo* (red bream), grilled to perfection. The best tables are on the quayside; the interior has a magnificent domed ceiling *(see also p67)*. *Rua da Ribeira 91 • Map E5 • (282) 461 592 • €*

9 O Charneco, Estômbar

Game, fish, meat and seafood make up the amazing 160 different dishes at this typical Algarve eatery. Culinary awards and caricatures of the proprietor adorn the walls. *Map E4 • Rua D. Sancho II, 3 • (282) 431 113 • €*

A Ruina, Albufeira

10 A Quinta, Almansil

Lively international menu, with surprises such as *assiete* of sea fish with Thai curry sauce. *Vale Formosa • Map J5 • (289) 393 357 • €€*

Left **Castro Marim** Centre **Tavira** Right **Alcoutim**

Eastern Region

LONG, NARROW SANDBANK ISLANDS stretch along much of the coastline of the eastern Algarve (Sotavento). These natural barriers shelter a fragile lagoon ecosystem that is home to a staggering variety of flora and fauna. Tucked behind them are timeworn fishing villages and hamlets. Further east, beautiful Renaissance churches loom over picturesque towns and elegant cities replete with Roman bridges, Moorish castles and the distinctive pyramid-shaped rooflines. The sparse interior is Nature's preserve, underlined by a culture and heritage that's remained unchanged for centuries.

Top 10 Sights

1. Tavira
2. Parque Natural da Ria Formosa
3. Castro Marim
4. Reserva Natural do Sapal
5. Alcoutim
6. Estói
7. Cacela Velha
8. Olhaõ
9. Vila Real de Santo António
10. Santa Luzia

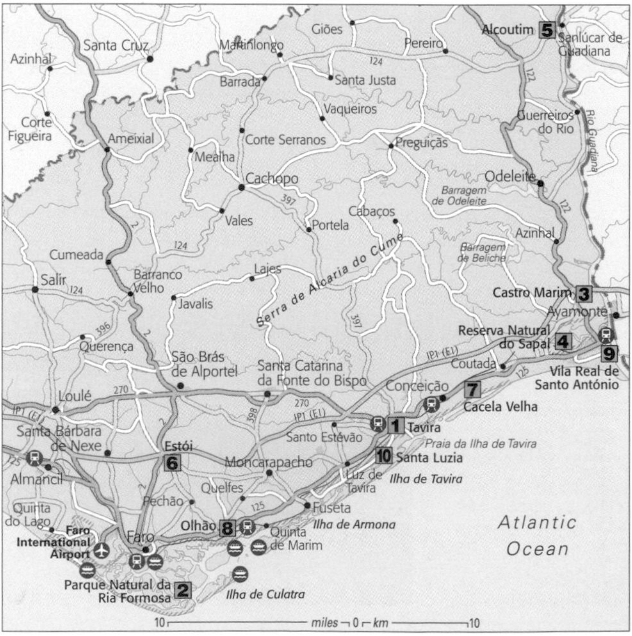

Moorish-style lattice door, Tavira

1 Tavira

Churches are emblematic of Tavira, with nearly 40 towers and spires piercing the town's skyline. Two are of great historical significance: the Igreja da Misericórdia, the Algarve's most important Renaissance monument; and the Igreja de Santa Maria do Castelo, final resting place of Dom Paio Peres Correia. The elegant Roman bridge spanning the River Gilão is another landmark that lends character to a town considered by many to be the most charming in the region *(see pp12–13)*.

2 Parque Natural da Ria Formosa

This vast realm of marshland, salinas and sand dune islands is home to the rare purple gallinule and the web-footed Portuguese water dog, among others. The lagoon habitat is one of the most important wetland zones in Europe. A purpose-built visitor centre houses an aquarium and exhibition area. Two exciting nature trails, São Lourenço and Quinta do Lago, provide excellent opportunities for observing wildlife at close quarters *(see pp24–7 & 50)*.

Reserva Natural do Sapal

3 Castro Marim

The timeworn frontier town of Castro Marim looms with genteel poise over the mouth of the River Guadiana, and its twin castles bear witness to the strategic importance the settlement played during centuries past. Grand views from the ramparts of the main 13th-century stronghold encompass the Reserva Natural do Sapal to the north and Vila Real de Santo António to the south. Spain shimmers in the distance *(see pp32–33)*.

4 Reserva Natural do Sapal

Much of this wetland park comprises working salt pans, but it's also a major winter feeding ground for spoonbill, greater flamingo, Kentish plover, avocet, black-winged stilt, Caspian tern and other birds. The visitor centre is located on the edge of the saltmarsh, and there's a lovely nature trail *(see p51)*.

Tavira

5 Alcoutim

The ramparts of a 14th-century castle still stand vigil over this delightful riverside hamlet nestling on the upper reaches of the River Guadiana. On the Spanish side, the equally slumbering village of Sanlúcar amounts to a mirror image of Alcoutim. Once upon a time these two neigbours were at war with each other and it was in the castle that Dom Fernando I of Portugal and his Spanish counterpart, Henrique II of Castile, signed a short-lived peace treaty in 1371. Boats regularly shuttle between the two villages. *Map P1 • Castle 9am–1pm, 2–5pm daily • Adm*

6 Estói

The quiet, unassuming country village of Estói basks in the glory of two major attractions. The pink Rococo façade of the town's florid, 19th-century palace holds court over a garden replete with ornamental fountains and a terrace decorated with blue and white azulejos. Ten minutes' walk away are the well preserved ruins of the Roman peristyle villa built in the 2nd century AD. *Map K5 • Estói Palace Gardens 9am–12:30pm, 2–5:30pm Tue–Sat • Free • Milreu Roman Ruins 9:30am–12:30pm, 2–5pm Mon–Sun (to 6pm in summer) • Adm*

Cacela Velha

Plucky Townsfolk of Olhão

In 1808, Olhão staged an uprising against the French garrison, which was the catalyst for Napoleon's retreat from Portuguese soil. In order to transmit the good news to King João VI in Brazil, a group of Olhão fishermen sailed to Rio de Janeiro, bereft of navigational charts. Their incredible voyage across the Atlantic so impressed the king that upon his return to the throne he elevated Olhão to town status.

7 Cacela Velha

Thought to have been a Phoenician settlement in origin, this quaint coastal hamlet commands one of the most unspoilt locations in the Algarve. A patchwork of fields and meadows surround a bluff crowned by an 18th-century fortress. Lying in its shadow is the parish church, its whitewashed candescence playing off the façades of the fishermen's cottages lining the tiny square. *Map N4*

Alcoutim

8 Olhaõ

One of the liveliest fishing ports in the Algarve has some fine seafood restaurants to match. The whole town revolves around fishing, a fact exemplified by the 17th-century parish church, built with donations from the local fishermen. At the chapel of Nossa Senhora dos Aflitos, women pray for the safe return of their menfolk during bad weather. The style of the town's cube-shaped houses, with flat roof terraces and external staircases, reflects the close trade links once enjoyed with North Africa. *Map L5*

9 Vila Real de Santo António

The original settlement here was submerged by monstrous tidal surges in the early 17th century. It was re-born in the late 18th century when the Marquês de Pombal designed a new town based on the Lisbon grid system. The town now attracts Spanish day trippers from Ayamonte, just over the River Guadiana, which in turn is a magnet for sightseers from Portugal *(see pp32–33)*.

Santa Luzia

10 Santa Luzia

Stunted palmeiras stud Santa Luzia's long esplanade, swaying lazily in the sea breezes. The village is synonymous with octopus, and dozens of empty *covos* (pots) can be seen stacked near the quay, the hapless contents of which are probably on the dinner table. Summer sea safaris depart from the quayside and cruise the waters off Ilha de Tavira. *Map M5*

A Drive to Alcoutim

Morning

A morning's drive north out of Castro Marim on the EN122 will take you through undulating hills, and lush valleys to the banks of the River Guadiana.

Allow a leisurely hour to get to **Alcoutim**. Ignore the sign for the town, which looms on your right just before Odeleite. (That will be the road for the return journey.) Instead, carry on past the Barragem de Odeleite, a huge shimmering reservoir, and snake past many hamlets until the junction at Cruzamento, where Alcoutim is signposted.

Refresh yourself at any one of Alcoutim's cafés hugging the central Praça da República. Alternatively, **O Soeiro** *(see p89)*, at the bottom of Rua Município, has an outside terrace near the quay.

Afternoon

After lunch, consider a mini-excursion to Spain. The local Portuguese *barqueiro* (boatman) will take passengers across the river to Sanlúcar, the mirror image of Alcoutim. An equally agreeable Spaniard will ferry you back when you're ready.

The drive back to Castro Marim, via the 507, is one of the most inspiring routes in the Algarve, along the bank of the Guadiana. Call in at the little Museu do Rio in **Guerreiros do Rio** *(p41)*, to find out about local life.

After Foz de Odeleite the road heads back to the hills before joining the EN122 and arrowing south.

Left **Praia de Manta Rota** Right **View of Ilha da Armona from Ria Formosa**

Top 10 Islands and Beaches

1 Ilha de Tavira
A huge offshore sandbank stretching 11 km (6 miles) west from Tavira, connected to land by a ferry from Quatro Águas. Alternatively, a mini railway can get you there from the resort of Pedras d'el Rei. *Map M5*

2 Ilha da Armona
Popular with independent travellers, the beaches facing inland are served by bars and restaurants. A ferry from Olhão takes 15 minutes. *Map L5–6*

3 Ilha da Culatra
The beaches here enjoy splendid isolation, and nude sunbathing in the dunes is not uncommon. The ferry takes 45 minutes from Olhão. *Map L–M5*

4 Ilha de Fuseta
You can walk onto this island at low tide, while the waters of the lagoon provide a popular venue for windsurfers. *Map M5*

5 Praia do Farol
A beautiful sweep of sand on the bank of a long sandspit island. Farol can be reached by a 45-minute ferry ride from the Porta Nova wharf below Faro's Old Town district. There are also departures from Olhão. *Map L6*

6 Ilha de Faro
This long sandy spit is reached by turning right off the main road just before Faro International Airport and walking across the causeway. It can get crowded in summer with Faro residents. *Map K6*

7 Praia do Ancão
A sublime beach opposite Quinta do Lago that narrows into a sand spit, the tip of which is the preserve of near-empty, tranquil dunes. *Map J6*

8 Ilha da Barreta
Boat departures from Faro's Porta Nova wharf shuttle visitors to this "deserted island", where wildlife can be observed. A bar-restaurant, O Estaminé, provides sustenance. *Map K6*

9 Praia de Cabanas
Less crowded than some of its neighbours, Cabanas' pristine beaches lie in peaceful seclusion and are reached by continuing westwards along the shores of Praia de Manta Rota. *Map N4*

Ilha de Faro

10 Praia de Manta Rota
Part of a sweep of golden sand that arches from Vila Real de Santo António to the tip of Praia de Cabanas. Access is via Manta Rota and Alagoas. *Map N4*

Previous pages **View from Alcoutim across the Guadiana to Spain**

Price Categories

For a three-course meal for one with half a bottle of wine (or equivalent meal), taxes and extra charges.

€	under €20
€€	€20–€30
€€€	€30–€40
€€€€	€40–€50
€€€€€	over €50

Left **O Patio** Right **O Ceú**

TOP 10 Places to Eat

1 Quatro Águas, Tavira

Inspiring lagoon views. Try the grilled lamb dish *costeletas de borrego na grelha "a murro"* *(see also p66)*. *Tavira • Map M4 • (281) 325 329 • No vegetarian dishes • €*

Monte Do Casal

2 O Patio, Tavira

Splendid, intimate eatery. House specialities include delicious *cataplana de pargo* (sea bream). *Rua António Cabreira 31, Tavira • Map M4 • (281) 323 008 • €*

3 Casa Velha, Cacela Velha

Set in one of the Algarve's prettiest hamlets, this quaint eatery attracts an enthusiastic Spanish clientele for its *feijoada de longueirão* (razor clams in bean stew) and other dishes. *Cacela Velha • Map N4 • (281) 952 297 • Closed Mon • No vegetarian dishes • €*

4 Monte do Casal, Estói

An old farmhouse restaurant with tempting fare, including a ravioli of goat's cheese with red pepper coulis. *Cerro do Lobo, Estói • Map K5 • (289) 991 503 • €€€€€*

5 Baixamar, Santa Luzia

This premier seafood restaurant is well known for its octopus, but the sautéed tuna is just as tempting. A photograph on the wall taken in 1954 shows Tavira under snow – an occurence unheard of since! *Avenida Duarte Pacheco, Santa Luzia • Map M5 • (281) 381 184 • No vegetarian dishes • €€*

6 O Ceú, Gorjões

The duck breast in sweet and sour sauce is marvellous, as is the deer in red wine. *Monte da Palhagueira, Gorjões, nr Santa de Barbara de Nexe • Map K5 • (289) 412 614 • No credit cards or vegetarian dishes • €€*

7 Restaurante Ria Formosa, Olhaõ

One local describes this much-loved restaurant as "an ocean under one roof". The menu bursts with catches such as fresh *besugos* (mullet). *Avenida 5 de Outubro, 14 • Map L5 • (289) 702 504 • No vegetarian dishes • €*

8 Os Arcos, Vila Real

A large, cavernous seafood restaurant on the town's riverfront. *Avenida da República, 45, Vila Real de Santo António • Map P4 • (281) 543 764 • No vegetarian dishes • €*

9 Luís dos Frangos, São Brás de Alportel

Down-to-earth establishment serving up succulent grilled chicken to an eager clientele. *Rua Dr José Dias Sanchos 134, São Brás de Alportel • Map K4 • (289) 842 635 • Closed Mon and through Sep • No vegetarian dishes • €*

10 Ti Afonso, Alcoutim

A taste of the river awaits those who opt for *caldeirada de enguias* (eel stew). *Praça da República, Alcoutim • Map P1 • (968) 425 975 • Closed Mon • No credit cards • No vegetarian options • €*

Left **Cabo de São Vicente** Centre **Vila Do Bispo** Right **Fishermen, Sagres**

Western Region

THE WESTERN ALGARVE (Barlavento) blends a precipitous Atlantic coastline with a verdant Mediterranean interior. The wild, windblown promontories associated with the legend of Henry the Navigator yield to forest-clad hills and cloud-tipped mountains. Some of the region's most spectacular beaches nestle on the south coast under outcrops of ochre-splashed rock. Others lie west to greet the surf that thunders onto the sand at the "end of the world". Underpinning the wonderful environmental fabric is a rich historical thread of Baroque churches and Manueline chapels, stark sea defences and baffling Neolithic monuments. Visitor attractions abound, with quaint restaurants in hushed villages waiting to be discovered, while lively resorts brushed by palm-lined avenues sway to a more cosmopolitan flavour.

Site of slave market, Lagos

Top 10 Sights

1. Lagos
2. Monchique and Caldas de Monchique
3. Sagres
4. Cabo de São Vicente
5. Parque Natural do Sudoeste Alentejano e Costa Vicentina
6. Aljezur
7. Vila do Bispo
8. Raposeira Chapel
9. Barragém da Bravura
10. Odeceixe

Cabo de São Vicente

1 Lagos

One of the most popular resort towns in southern Portugal, Lagos immediately captures the imagination with its carefree holiday spirit, laid-back lifestyle and immense historical wealth. Its greatest treasure is the Igreja de Santo António. The nearby beaches are equally attractive with their fine golden sand, ochre-splashed cliffs and bizarre outcrops of sandstone pillars *(see pp20–23)*.

2 Monchique and Caldas de Monchique

Monchique, a rustic little market town, is tucked away in the forested Serra de Monchique under a mantle of towering eucalyptus and broad magnolia. Nestling in its shadow is Caldas de Monchique, a charming leafy hamlet glowing in the fame of its renowned spa facility where the sparkling mineral water is endowed with some remarkable curative properties. The Serra's unique Mediterranean-Atlantic habitat is a haven for wildlife. Sweeping views from Fóia and Picota crown this hugely diverse and fertile area *(see pp16–17)*.

3 Sagres

Sagres's claim to fame is the huge landmark fort spread across the arm of the precipitous Ponta de Sagres. It's here that Henry the Navigator's original fortress and the Vila do Infante – his legendary school of navigation – is said to have been located. Little remains of either except for the giant pebble Rosa dos Ventos (wind compass) and the plain little chapel of Nossa Senhora da Graça, both supposedly used by Henry in the 15th century. Sagres itself is a modest town bestowed with a pretty harbour and some magnificent beaches that attract surfers from around the globe *(see pp28–9)*.

4 Cabo de São Vicente

An austere landscape, dramatic limestone cliffs and a restless, unforgiving sea led Greek chroniclers to describe this windblown cape as the end of the earth. The Romans revered the rocky outcrop and called it Promontorium Sacrum, a place where the setting sun hissed in its dying embers as the ocean swallowed it up. The promontory retains an air of mystique. The cape's lighthouse is an important navigation reference point and looms over a former convent building. Henry the Navigator is said to have had a house in the small castle to the right of the tower. *Map B5*

Monchique

5 Parque Natural do Sudoeste Alentejano e Costa Vicentina

The entire coastline of western Algarve lies within the boundaries of this wild and rocky nature reserve. Dozens of scarce and endemic plant species thrive here, and the highly secretive Iberian lynx stalks the land. Hundreds of different species of birdlife flutter and glide above the salt marshes, while, not surprisingly, ornithologists gather with binoculars primed.

Map B5 • Park office, Rua João Dias Mendes 46-A, Aljezur • (282) 998 673

6 Aljezur

The humble ruins of a 10th-century Moorish castle stand sentinel-like over a higgledy-piggeldy collection of whitewashed houses and café-restaurants that constitute the village of Aljezur. A steep, cobbled path leads up to the timeworn but sturdy castle walls and the splendid view beyond. This riverine area was once a breeding ground for malaria-carrying mosquitoes, and in the 18th century some of the villagers were persuaded to relocate to Igreja Nova, Aljezur's "modern" counterpart to the east. *Map C3*

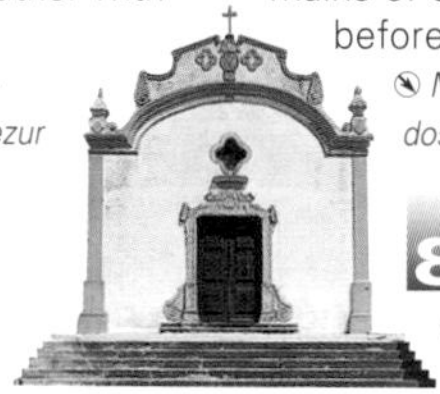

Vila do Bispo

7 Vila do Bispo

The landscape around Vila do Bispo is rich with evidence of the Algarve's prehistoric past. Mysterious *menhirs*, also known as megaliths, dot the countryside. Near Monte dos Amantes, a number of these stones, some bearing crudely carved crosses, appear to form a circle. Archaeologists speculate this could be the site of the mythical Church of the Raven, supposedly where the remains of St Vincent were interred before being taken to Lisbon.

Map B5 • Menhir circuit, Monte dos Amantes, Vila do Bispo

8 Raposeira

Considered to be one of the oldest examples of Gothic architecture in the Algarve, this unassuming 14th-century chapel is of great significance. Henry the Navigator was said to have prayed here when he lived in the nearby town of Raposeira, as did many a crew before departing for unknown lands. Inside the chapel, built in honour of the Virgin of Guadalupe, enigmatic stone heads peer down from the ceiling.

Map B5 • EN 125, Raposeira • 9:30am–5pm Wed–Sat, Tue & Sun afternoons only • Closed last weekend of every month

Aljezur

Barragém da Bravura

9 Barragém da Bravura

The huge, man-made lake 10 km (6 miles) north of Lagos is a wonderful place to unpack the picnic hamper. In spring, fields of orchids nestle under delicate umbrellas of almond blossom, with butterflies flitting from bloom to bloom. Towering eucalyptus encroach upon the lakeside, and the woods are a favourite haunt of red foxes and wild boar. The higher ground north of the dam is generously wooded with cork oak, and it's from this area that the best views of the lake can be enjoyed.

Map D4

10 Odeceixe

The River Seixe meanders past this pretty little village, which makes a handy base for surfers keen to ride the big swells that thunder onto Odeceixe beach. A lone windmill sitting above the village used to take advantage of the fresh winds whipped up by the Atlantic; today it's a popular spot for scanning the Alentejo countryside. There's also a curious little museum in the village centre, which recreates the atmosphere of a traditional winery and cellar. This sleepy backwater is about as far as you can get from the summer throngs that pack the coastal resorts.

Map C1 • Windmill 10am–noon, 1–4pm Mon–Fri • Museum 7pm–11pm Wed–Sun

A Tour of the West

Morning

Breakfast in **Lagos** *(see p91)* can be enjoyed at the café in Praça Infante Dom Henrique near the castle walls, before you set out to explore the west coast.

The drive follows the EN125, crossing the boundary of the **Parque Natural do Sudoueste Alentejano e Costa Vicentina**. The road winds on – via the tiny 14th-century chapel of Nossa Senhora da Guadalupe and the prehistoric sights of **Vila do Bispo** – to **Sagres** *(p91)* and its landmark 17th-century fort.

For an invigorating walk and to further appreciate the seascape at Sagres, follow the path around the promontory.

By now, it should be time for refreshments at Café-Restaurante Cochina on Praça da República or, if you prefer something more substantial, the Restaurante Atlântico on Rua Comandante Matoso.

Afternoon

Sagres has a pretty harbour which can be investigated on foot. Perched on a bluff overlooking the fishing boats are the ruins of Fortaleza da Baleeira which can be reached by turning up onto the dirt track off the roundabout near the quay.

No trip to the west coast would be complete without a visit to **Cabo de São Vicente** *(p91)* which is a short drive northwest. The clifftop vistas are truly awe-inspiring and a suitably dramatic way to end the day's sightseeing.

Left **Praia do Armado, Carrapateira** Centre **Meia Praia, Lagos** Right **Praia de Odeceixe**

Top 10 Beaches

1 Praia de Dona Ana, Lagos
A spectacular and intimate picture-postcard beach, framed by extraordinary outcrops of ochre sandstone. A warren of caves and grottoes runs through the base of the nearby cliff face. *Map D5*

2 Praia do Armado, Carrapateira
One of the surfer's favourites, Armado's Atlantic swells attract enthusiasts keen to ride the surf back into the wide sweeping beach. *Map B4*

3 Praia de Odeceixe
The River Seixe runs into this delightfully secluded stretch of sand, tucked away right up in the northern reaches of the Algarve, close to the Alentejo border. *Map C1*

4 Praia de Figueira, Salema
This popular beach fronts the tidy fishing village of Salema and attracts a young, sporty crowd, with windsurfing running a close second to sunbathing. *Map C5*

5 Meia Praia, Lagos
At 4 km (2 miles), this is one of the longest beaches in the Algarve, with plenty of room for sunbathers to share the sand with water-skiers and windsurfers. *Map D5*

6 Praia de Burgau
One of the best locations in the area for snorkelling and diving, the beach skirts Burgau resort and is hemmed in on either side by sloping cliffs. *Map C5*

7 Praia do Martinhal
Another fabulous location for windsurfing, with the ocean lapping a golden swathe of sand. The beach is also conveniently situated near the town of Sagres. *Map B6*

8 Praia do Beliche
The steep climb down a cliff path to the beach is rewarded with a wonderfully secluded wedge of pristine sand that sees few visitors because of its somewhat awkward location. *Map B5*

9 Praia da Luz
A fine beach with very easy access to resort amenities, Luz can get crowded mid-season. But there's always some room, especially towards its eastern flank. *Map C5*

Praia de Dona Ana, Lagos

10 Praia de Monte Clérigo
Another preferred beach of the surfing set and tourists possessed of a more independent spirit. An isolated landscape with untamed breakers. *Map C2*

Previous pages **Terraced farmland, Monchique**

Left **Canoes at Martinhal** Centre **Surfboarder** Right **Coastal walkers**

Top 10 Outdoor Pursuits

1 Horse Riding
With its almond and cork oak trees, the countryside around Bensafrim, northwest of Lagos, makes for idyllic riding territory. *Quinta do Paraiso Alto riding centre, Fronteira • Map C4 • (282) 687 596*

2 Diving
Ponta de Sagres is one of the best dive sites on the Iberian peninsula, with its network of tunnels and caverns and, 2 km (1 mile) offshore, the rusty shell of a WW1 freighter. *Scubado Algarve, Porto da Baleeira, Apartado 28, Sagres • Map B6 • (282) 624 549*

3 Bird Watching
The Cabo de São Vicente headland offers a superb vantage from which to observe birds in spring and autumn, when the skies are dotted with eagles, storks, sparrowhawks, griffon and Egyptian vultures. *Map B5*

4 Surfing
The Atlantic rollers pummelling Praia do Armado lure many surfers. Competitions take place throughout summer. *Map B4*

5 Hiking
Serra da Monchique provides the most demanding walking. Wooded foothills give way to a treeless summit speckled with rhododendron blooms. The views fully justify the long hike. *Map D2*

6 Coastal Walks
A favourite is the footpath from Luz to Burgau. It starts in open countryside, follows the coastline along the lip of a cliff, then slopes to the sea. *Map C5*

7 Big Game Fishing
Warm coastal waters (Jun–Sep) attract marlin and sharks. Sports fishermen usually return triumphant from the "fighting chair". *Espadarte do Sul, Doca Pesca No.4, Lagos • Map D5 • (282) 767 252*

8 Freshwater Kayaking
Barragem de Bravura is a huge, tree-fringed reservoir, and a kayak safari is the best way to observe its diverse wildlife. *Blue Ocean Diving & Kayak Centre, Lagos • Map D4 • (282) 782 718*

9 Ancient Archaeology Tour
Dating back at least 5,000 years, *menhirs* stud the area around the village of Vila do Bispo *(see p92)*. *Menhir circuit, Monte dos Amantes, Vila do Bispo • Map B5*

10 Nature Safaris
Specialist guides can help you appreciate fully places such as the Parque Natural do Alentejano e Costa Vicentina, a beautiful and rugged landscape of cliffs, isolated beaches and undulating hills. *Horizonte jeep safaris, Salema • Map B5 • (282) 695 920*

Archaeological tour

Left **Zambezi Art Gallery** Right **Crocheted dolls, Cabo de São Vicente Lighthouse**

Top 10 Places to Shop

1 Rua Cândido dos Reis / Rua 25 de Abril, Lagos

The busiest streets in town, where shoppers can browse the rows of stores and boutiques for jewellery, handicrafts and fashion. *Map D5*

2 Casa dos Arcos

One of the few places in the Algarve where you can purchase *cadeiras de tesoura*, the folding wooden chairs, which are hand-crafted to an ancient Roman design. *José Salvador, Estrada Velha, Monchique • Map E3*

Casa dos Arcos

3 Mediconforto

Cavernous health food shop with a huge selection of minerals, vitamins, homeopathic remedies and natural cosmetics. *Rua Silva Costa, Lagos • Map D5*

4 Atelier Opalina

A stunning range of handmade jewellery fashioned out of gold, silver, mother-of-pearl and precious stones. *Praça do Infante, 1, Lagos • Map D5*

5 Jerome Gay

Half Spanish, half English, Jerome Gay is a cutting-edge artist of *azulejos* (painted ceramic tiles) who has taken this traditional art form to a new level of sophistication. His studio in Pereira, in the foothills of Monchique, is also a gallery. *(282) 471 446 or (965) 049 722 for directions • Map E3*

6 São Vicente Giftshop

The place to shop for quality linen and colourful ceramics. Also a bookshop of sorts and snack bar. *Estrada do Farol, Sagres • Map B6*

7 Cabo de São Vicente Lighthouse Crochet Workshop

Baskets full of crocheted bootees, pin cushions, coasters and table mats, all intricately woven in white and embellished with colourful decoration. *Cabo de São Vicente, Vila do Bispo • Map B5*

8 Aljezur Gypsy Market

A lively gypsy troupe trundles into Aljezur on the third Monday of every month with an extraordinary array of clothing, household items and foodstuffs at bargain prices. *Map C3*

9 Barão de São João Flea Market

Jolly open-air antiques market and handicrafts fair on the fourth Sunday of every month. *Barão de S.João • Map C4 • 9am–5pm*

10 Zambezi Art Gallery

A celebration of all things African, this gallery displays a wealth of artifacts and offers a stunning range for sale, including Congolese beer coolers and Nigerian wood sculpture. *Rua do Baluarte, Loja C. Lote 31, Lagos • Map D5*

Price Categories

For a three-course meal for one with half a bottle of wine (or equivalent meal), taxes and extra charges.

€	under €20
€€	€20–€30
€€€	€30–€40
€€€€	€40–€50
€€€€€	over €50

Left **Barroca** Right **Mullens**

TOP 10 Places to Eat

1 Adega Vilalisa, Mexilhoeira Grande

A rural gem with fine traditional cuisine, including succulent pork knee roast *(see also p66)*. *52 Rua Francisco Bivar, Mexilhoeira Grande • Map D4 • (282) 968 478 • No vegetarian dishes • €*

2 Barroca, Lagos

Viva Mexico! Indulge yourself with big nachos topped with chilli con carne *(see also p67)*. *Rua da Barroca, 1, Lagos • Map D5 • (282) 767 162 • No credit cards • €*

3 Mullens, Lagos

Full of character and run by a young, friendly staff. The spicy beef, Mozambique-style, is incredible. *Rua Cândido Reis, 86, Lagos • Map D5 • (282) 761 281 • No credit cards • No vegetarian dishes • €*

4 Adega Papagaio, Espiche

Choose from seven different meats, all chargrilled on a hot stone. *Rua da Adega, Espiche, nr Lagos • Map D5 • (282) 789 423 • €*

5 Cabrita, Carrapateira

The proprietor is equally proud of his fresh fish and an autograph by late Beatle George Harrison, scribbled on a one-dollar bill. *8670-230 Bordeira Carrapateira • Map B4 • (282) 973 128 • No credit cards • No vegetarian dishes • €*

6 Fortaleza, Praia da Luz

A 16th-century fortress with fabulous views and *espetada de frango* (chicken kebabs) among other delights. *Rua da Igreja 1, Praia da Luz • Map C5 • (282) 789 926 • €€€*

7 Bica Boa, Monchique

Opt for the terrace during fine weather for a wholesome *al fresco* treat in idyllic surrounds. *Estrada de Lisboa, 266, Monchique • Map E3 • (282) 912 271 • €*

8 O Chefe Dimas, Aljezur

The *tamboril* (monkfish) is a speciality, and the home-made desserts are scrumptious. *North of Aldeia Velha, Aljezur • Map C3 • (282) 998 275 • Closed Wed • No credit cards • No vegetarian dishes • €*

9 Dormidas, Odeceixe

Try the *borrego estufado* (stewed lamb) or *robala* (sea perch). *Rua Nova, 20, Odeceixe • Map C1 • (282) 947 352 • No vegetarian dishes • €*

10 Fortaleza do Beliche, Sagres

Arguably one of the most romantic settings in the Algarve, offering traditional Portuguese fare. *Cabo de São Vicente-Sagres, Sagres • Map B5 • (282) 624 124 • No vegetarian dishes • €€*

Adega Vilalisa

Left **Lusitano horse** Centre **Monsaraz rooftops** Right **Granite figures in Évora**

The Alentejo

UNDULATING PLAINS *and blistering summer heat characterize much of this province to the north of the Algarve. Blankets of yellow wheat sway across huge tracts of land, and much of the sun-baked earth is pocked by stubby cork and olive trees. Vines trace emerald lines across ochre soil to surround whitewashed villages. To the north, medieval settlements perch on steep, granite escarpments in an altogether rockier terrain. While, down by the coast, secluded beaches of golden sand brush sleepy, unhurried resorts that wake up in summer, when the days are long and the air is warm.*

Top 10 Sights of the Alentejo

1. Évora
2. Marvão
3. Mértola
4. Monsaraz
5. Castelo de Vide
6. Vila Viçosa
7. Beja
8. Estremoz
9. Elvas
10. Serpa

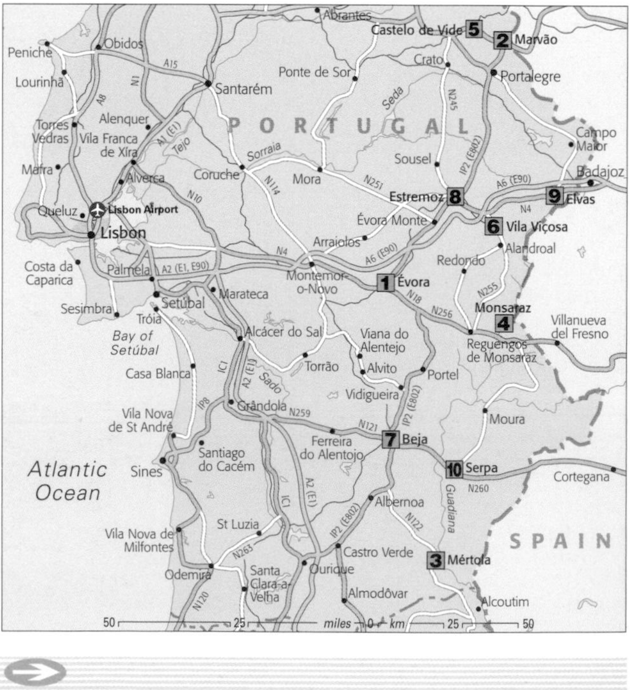

Praça do Giraldo in Évora

1 Évora

The historic centre of Évora, capital of the Alentejo, is listed as a UNESCO World Heritage Site. Stunning examples of Roman, Moorish, medieval and 17th-century architecture abound in the narrow streets and breezy squares. The central Praça do Giraldo has a wonderful 16th-century fountain. A walk from the square up the lively Rua 5 de Outubro leads to the grandiose Sé (cathedral). An adjacent 16th-century palace houses the Museu de Évora. The nearby Roman temple is the best preserved monument of its kind in Portugal. *(See the itinerary on p103).* *Tourist info: Praça do Giralde 65 • (266) 702 671*

2 Marvão

Named "the eagle's nest" by locals, this medieval hamlet, set high upon on a rugged escarpment, is an astonishing sight. Sinuous 13th-century battlements envelope an immaculate village, where polished cobbled streets snake past neat façades, whitewashed cottages, a dainty church, trim gardens and a cherished museum. Crowning all this is a castle commanding dramatic views of the Serra de Marvão and the borderlands. *Tourist info: Largo de Santa Maria • (245) 993 886*

3 Mértola

Designated a *vila museu*, or open-air museum-town, the old quarter of Mértola is divided into a number of areas of historic interest. Each reflects the diverse periods in the town's history: Phoenicians, Romans, Visigoths and Moors all took advantage of its strategic position on the River Guadiana. A number of museums exhibit treasures from each period, but the most stunning collection can be found in the new Museu Islâmico. *Tourist info: Rua Alonso Gomes • (286) 612 573*

4 Monsaraz

Swathes of vineyards surround Monsaraz, a name synonymous with some of the finest Portuguese wine. The fortified hilltop village is a delight, especially in spring when bright red poppies cling to the granite walls of the 13th-century castle. Also highly visible are the twin bell towers of the Igreja Matriz, holding court over a maze of truncated lanes lined with squat dwellings and tucked-away restaurants. *Tourist info: Largo Dom Nuno Álvares Pereira • (266) 557 136*

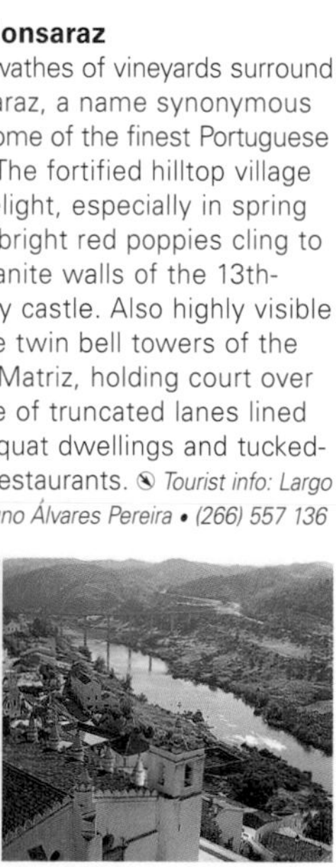

Left **View from Marvão's castle** Right **Mértola**

Right **Castelo de Vide** Centre **Paço Ducal, Vila Viçosa**

5 Castelo de Vide

The old Jewish quarter is the most enjoyable part of this attractive spa town. It stretches away from the 13th-century castle that gives the town its name in a cluster of steep lanes, many sporting plaques testifying to the quality of their floral displays. A synagogue (also 13th-century) sits at the top of this stepped thoroughfare, which also leads down to the 16th-century marble Fonte da Vila. *Tourist info: Rua Bartolomeu A. da Santa 81 • (245) 901 361*

6 Vila Viçosa

During the 15th century Vila Viçosa became the country seat of the dukes of Bragança and the town is best known today for its splendid Paço Ducal. The semi-ruined battlements of the dukes' former abode, the castle, surround a collection of brightly painted cottages and the 14th-century church of Nossa Senhora da Conceição. *Tourist info: Praça da República • (268) 881 101*

7 Beja

A thriving agricultural town and capital of the Baixo Alentejo, Beja also has a rich past displayed in museum buildings that are often as interesting as their exhibits. The Convento de Nossa Senhora da Conceição, for example, now houses the Museu Regional, and the town's oldest church, the 6th-century Santo Amaro, is home to the Museu Visigótico. The landmark Torre de Menagem (castle keep) dates from the late 13th century. *Tourist info: Rua Capitão João Francisco de Sousa 25 • (284) 311 913*

8 Estremoz

Dominating this graceful town is the Torre das Três Coroas, the Tower of the Three Crowns, named in honour of kings Sancho II, Afonso III and Dinis. You can gain free access to the tower via the adjoining castle and palace. The nearby Museu Municipal is housed in a 17th-century almshouse. Among the exhibits are some wonderful examples of *bonecos*, pottery figurines typical of

Chapter house, Beja's Museu Regional

Aqueduct between Amoreira and Elvas

the region. *Tourist info: Largo da República 26 • (268) 333 541*

9 Elvas

Chunky pentagonal bastions, thick walls and gaping moats surround this busy frontier town near the Spanish border. The 17th-century fortifications resemble a multifaceted star and are very well preserved – they are best viewed from the castle. Within the walls are the excellent Museu Municipal and Biblioteca and the tiny 16th-century church of Nossa Senhora dos Aflitos. The mighty Aqueduto da Amoreira stretches between Elvas and a spring some 5 miles (8 km) away at Amoreira. *Tourist info: Tourist info: Praça da República • (268) 622 236*

10 Serpa

This tranquil town makes for leisurely exploration. Start with the city walls and the stout towers of the Porta de Beja. Up above are the remains of an 11th-century aqueduct. Within the walls the castle provides the strongest focal point, and its ramparts offer sweeping views of the Alentejan plains. Finally, leave time to sample some *queijo de Serpa*, a creamy ewe's milk cheese often served as a starter. *Tourist info: Largo Dom Jorge de Melo 2–3 • (284) 544 727*

A Day in Évora

Morning

Begin at the **Praça do Giraldo** and wander up Rua 5 de Outubro towards the **Sé (cathedral)**. Look out for the 14th-century carved Apostles flanking the portal and, once inside, climb to the treasury to see the 13th-century ivory figure of the Virgin.

Adjacent to the cathedral is the **Museu de Évora**, where a dazzling 16th-century Flemish polyptych, *Life of the Virgin*, can be found upstairs.

On the opposite side of the square are the granite Corinthian columns of the **Templo Romano** – the best-preserved Roman monument in Portugal.

From here, retrace your steps back to Praça do Giraldo for lunch or a coffee at **Café Cozinha de Santo Humberto**.

Afternoon

Take Rua da República, on the eastern side of Praça do Giraldo. A few minutes' walk brings you to Praça 1 de Maio lorded over by the huge 16th-century Manueline-Gothic **Igreja de São Francisco**.

The church's principal draw is the **Capela dos Ossos (Chapel of Bones)**. The skeletal remains of some 5,000 monks line the walls and columns of the chapel. An inscription above the entrance reads, *"Nós ossos que aqui estamos, pelos vossos esperamos"* ("We bones that are here await yours").

Time to rest, maybe back at one of the cafés on Praça do Giraldo.

Following pages **Bull fight, Monsaraz castle**

Left **Serra do São Mamede** Centre **Cromlech of Almendres** Right **Monastery, Crato**

TOP 10 Best of the Rest

1 Viana do Alentejo
A little backwater famed for its natural springs, but also home to a fine 14th-century castle and a fortified church. Peacocks roam round the pilgrim church of Nossa Senhora de Aires, 20 minutes' walk east of the town centre.

2 Serra de Sâo Mamede
This beautiful and diverse nature reserve is home to a stunning variety of wildlife: Bonelli's eagle, Egyptian vulture, genet and the Iberian midwife toad are some of the residents.

3 Cromlech of Almendres (Guadalupe)
The Cromlech of Almendres stone circles are considered the most important megalith group in the Iberian peninsula. Nearby is the Neolithic Dolmen of Zambujeiro.

4 Vila Nova de Milfontes
An attractive seaside resort hugging the River Mira near a vast swathe of golden sand. Popular in summer, with superb surf.

5 Portalegre
The superb Museu do Guy Fino (named in honour of the founder of Portalegre's last remaining tapestry factory) showcases some of the finest examples of tapestry in Europe.

6 Évoramonte
Dramatic views reward those who make it to Évoramonte's castle walls which are embellished with curious stone "ropes". Dom Miguel ceded the throne in Évoramonte on 26 May 1834.

7 Arraiolos/Pavia
The foundations of the castle at Arraiolos date back to Celtic times, while in Pavia, 18 km (11 miles) to the north, a tiny chapel has been built into a dolmen – architecturally unique in Portugal.

8 Crato
Neat rows of whitewashed houses with yellow trim characterize this town, once the headquarters of the 14th-century Order of Hospitallers. Exhibits in the Museu Municipal explain more about Crato's illustrious past.

Folk crucifix, Portalegre

9 Redondo
Dozens of hole-in-the-wall *olarias* (pottery workshops) line the narrow streets of Redondo, which makes it a worthy stop-off to pick up a slew of ceramic souvenirs.

10 Zambujeira do Mar
An annual rock festival has put this coastal smudge of a village resort on the map, but its secluded beach and other-world charm has always attracted the more independent of travellers.

Left **Rua 5 de Outubro, Évora** Right **Locally grown vegatables, Alentejo**

Top 10 Places to Shop

1 Rua 5 de Outubro, Évora
Lined with *artesanatos* (handicrafts shops) bristling with ceramics, carved cork, copper *cataplanas* (cooking pots), hand-painted chairs, occasional tables and other curios. On the second Tuesday of every month a lively open-air market takes place across the Rossio de São Brás, just outside the town walls.

2 Rua de Cima 7, Marvão
An incongruous but very useful minimarket, squeezed in between rows of stone cottages, caters to residents and self-catering travellers alike. There are also one or two *artesanatos* in the same street.

3 Loja Astrolabio, Mértola
A fantastic collection of handmade ceramic art and reproductions of Phoenician, Roman and medieval glass artifacts. *Rua Alonso Gomes, 10*

4 Coisas de Monsaraz
Homemade jams and other assorted knick-knacks can be bought from this friendly little arts and craft shop nestling in the shadows of the castle walls. *Largo do Castelo 2, Monsaraz*

5 Charcutaria, Castelo de Vide
Bottles of wine, honey, sweets and cakes, and spicy sausages make up some of the regional goodies for sale in this traditional *loja* (shop). *Rua de Olivença, 29*

6 Mercado Municipal, Vila Viçosa
Housed is a modern complex in the town centre, the market is at its busiest early on Saturday mornings when it overflows with fresh fruit and vegetables, and a wide selection of fish. *Largo D. João IV • 9am–1pm, daily*

7 Rua Afonso Costa, Beja
A narrow, atmospheric precinct lined with fashion boutiques, traditional handicrafts shops and cafés.

8 Antiquedades, Estremoz
Beautiful and original antiques fill this small shop near the Torre das Três Coroas in the old quarter. The Saturday market (in the lower town, across the Rossio) is the place to buy goat's and ewe's milk cheeses and the famous preserved plums.

9 Rua de Alcamim, Elvas
A busy pedestrianized street with florists, music stores, shoe shops and the usual handicrafts. The weekly Monday market takes place near the impressive Aqueduto da Amoreira.

10 Turismo, Serpa
The tourist office has a great selection of traditional chairs, jars of honey and colourful house façades fashioned in miniature. On the fourth Tuesday of every month a country market is hosted on the outskirts of the town. *Turismo, Largo Dom Jorge de Melo, 2*

Left **Selection of wines** Right **The wine-producing region of Vidigueira**

Top 10 Top Ten Alentejan Wines

1 Marquês de Borba Reserva 1999 (Tinto)

Robust red from the João Ramos Portugal stable. Blended from periquita, aragonês and trincadeira grape varieties and matured in French oak, this deep crimson delight enhances casseroles and roasts.

2 Esporão Garrafeira 1997 (Tinto)

Complex wine showing ripe fruit and well-integrated oak characters with rich, textured tannins, superb balance and long, flavoursome aftertaste. A perfect match with hearty, Alentejan fare.

3 Quinta do Mouro 1997 (Tinto)

Harmonious blend of ripe fruit flavours with a jolly 14 per cent alcohol content. Deep crimson with rich, oak finish and full-bodied bouquet. Enjoy with game.

4 Herdade Grande Colheita Selecionada Branco 2000 (Branco)

A delicious wine with ripe, aromatic peach and melon fruits. Rich, full palate with creamy texture and soft finish. Wonderful with baked fish, salad or chicken.

5 Esporão Touriga Nacional 1999 (Tinto)

Has typical violet and dark berry fruit aromas with toasty oak complexity. Palate is firm with rich spicy fruit characters. Complements pastas and red meat.

6 Dolium Regional Alentejano Branco 2000 (Branco)

Made exclusively from the Alentejo's top white grape variety, antão vaz, to produce a wine of citrus colour with fragrant toast and vanilla spice aromas. Superb with fish dishes.

7 Cortes de Cima 1999 (Tinto)

Dark and concentrated in colour with a ripe, red-berry-and-cherry aroma enhanced by subtle hints of spicy French and American oak. Excellent with steak and game.

8 Vila Santa 1998 (Tinto)

A deep violet wine made from trincadeira, aragonês, cabernet sauvignon and alicante bouschet grape varieties. Smooth on the palate and a healthy companion with *javoli* (wild boar).

9 Outeiro 2000 (Branco)

Soft white that shows a spicy aroma of tropical fruits. Made from the roupeiro, arinto and antão vaz grape varieties. Ideal chilled as an aperitif.

10 Monsaraz 2000 (Tinto)

Ruby in hue with a complex aroma of ripe blackberry and cherry. Smooth, soft and rounded, and an all-round favourite.

Price Categories

For a three-course meal for one with half a bottle of wine (or equivalent meal), taxes and extra charges.

€	under €20
€€	€20–€30
€€€	€30–€40
€€€€	€40–€50
€€€€€	over €50

Left **O Alentejano** Right **Cabrito assado (roast kid), a favourite dish of rural Portugal**

TOP 10 Places to Eat

1 Fialho
Specialities include *cacão de coentrada* (dog fish with coriander sauce). Advance booking is essential. *Travessa dos Mascarenhas 16, Évora • (266) 703 079 • Closed Mon • €€*

Fialho restaurant sign

2 São Rosas
Superb location right in front of the Torre das Três Coroas, matched by first-class service. Great puddings. *Largo D. Dinis 11, Estremoz • (268) 333 345 • €€*

3 Restaurante Casa do Povo
Sweeping terrace views in one of Portugal's most beautiful mountain villages makes dining here a real treat. The *bifes de vitela* (veal steaks) are particularly recommended. *Travessa do Chabouco, Marvão • (245) 993 160 • €*

4 Migas
Wonderfully unassuming with friendly service, Migas is one of the few restaurants to serve traditional *sopas de poejo com entrecosto* (soup with fried meat). *Mercado Municipal, Mértola • (286) 612 811 • No Credit Cards • €*

5 O Alcaide
Discreetly wedged in between a row of cottages, this homely eatery radiates warmth and relaxed hospitality. Excellent regional fare and a generous wine list. *Rua de Santiago 18, Monsaraz • (266) 557 168 • Closed Thu • €*

6 O Alentejano
A firm favourite with locals at lunchtime. Ask for the superb-value "Dish of the Day". *Largo dos Mártires da República 14, Castelo de Vide • (245) 901 355 • No Credit Cards • €*

7 Os Cucos
Set in verdant, shady gardens, with a daily-changing menu that errs towards earthy Alentejan fare. There's an outside terrace for coffee and snacks. *Mata Municipal, Vila Viçosa • (268) 980 806 • €*

8 Teotonius
Arched ceilings and low lights provide a romantic setting for this cosy restaurant. The imaginative menu includes diet-inducing fondue. *Rua do Touro 8, Beja • (284) 328 010 • No Credit Cards • Closed Mon • €*

9 Restaurante Alentejano
Order the *ensopado de borrego a pastora* (lamb stew shepherdess' style) for a real taste of the Alentejo. *Praça da República, Serpa • (284) 544 335 • €*

10 O Lagar
Popular with locals and tourists alike, bustling O Lagar dishes up choice fare, including *bacalhau à lagar* (codfish Lagar style). Its central location ensures a busy turnaround. *Rua Nova da Vedoria 11, Elvas • (268) 624 793 • No Credit Cards • Closed Thu • €*

ALBUFEIRA
CARTE D'OR
Olá
PIZZARIA

STREETSMART

Left **Road sign** Centre **Faro airport** Right **Ferry, Vila Real de Santo António**

Top 10 Getting to the Algarve

1 Visa and Entry Requirements

You will need a valid passport to enter Portugal, but no visa is required for EU nationals. Those arriving from Canada, New Zealand or the USA can stay for a maximum of 90 days in any half-year without a visa.

2 By Air From Within Europe

The entry/exit point for visitors by plane is Faro International Airport. The national airline, TAP Air Portugal, and domestic airline Portugalia operate daily scheduled services between Faro and Lisbon and Oporto. There are connections with many international flights out of Lisbon.

3 By Air From the Rest of the World

Faro International Airport serves both domestic and foreign carriers, all of which arrive and depart from the same terminal. During the high season the airport gets very busy, and even those travelling business class can expect ticket and customs delays.

4 Faro Airport

The airport is located 6 km (3 miles) outside the town, but airline ticket holders can use the free Aerobus shuttle into Faro. The bus runs between mid-May and November and has its own parking bay outside the arrivals hall. All the major car hire companies have offices at the airport.

5 By Road From Lisbon

A tolled motorway links the Portuguese capital, Lisbon, with the Algarve. Ordinarily, this journey will take around three hours, but in summer long queues form at the toll booths. An alternative route is the toll-free IC1, which runs parallel to the IP1 and IP2.

6 By Road from Spain

The Ayamonte-Huelva toll-free motorway links the Algarve with the Spanish towns of Seville, Córdoba and Madrid.

7 By Scenic Coastal and/or Hill Route

An alternative way to drive to the Algarve from Lisbon is by following the IC1 as far as Mimosa and then turning onto the N263 towards Odemira. Carry on through this town to the N120 which follows the boundaries of the Parque Natural do Sudoeste Alentejano e Costa Vicentina. This wonderfully scenic route will eventually take you all the way to Lagos but will add at least another hour onto your journey time. Another way is to come off the N263 before Odemira and follow the N266 to Monchique – a long and winding, but very pretty drive.

8 By Bus/Coach

There are excellent express coach services to Faro from towns and cities right across Portugal. The two main coach companies are EVA Transportes SA and Renex. It is best to pre-book tickets from the main bus stations.

9 By Air via Local Aerodromes

The Algarve is served by two aerodromes at Alvor, near Portimão, and Lagos. Private jets and light airplanes also fly in and out of Faro. Alvor and Lagos aerodromes operate sightseeing tours and flight instruction as well.

10 Boat

The marinas at Lagos, Vilamoura and Albufeira serve the international yachting community, but for those without a boat there is a ferry service that connects Vila Real de Santo António, in the Algarve, with the Spanish town of Ayamonte, Alcoutim and Sanlúcar.

Directory

General Flight Information
(289) 800 801 • Faro Airport • Map K6

Alvor Aerodrome
Near Portimão • (282) 495 828

Lagos Aerodrome
(282) 762 906

Previous pages **Rua 5 de Outubro, Albufeira**

Left **Taxis** Centre **Regional train** Right **Cyclists, Praia do Armado**

TOP 10 Getting Around the Algarve

1 By Road

The road system in the Algarve is generally very good, though the main routes are busy in summer and many back roads are no more than dirt tracks – a four-wheel drive is sometimes required in the hills.

2 Rules of the Road

Driving is on the right. The speed limit through towns and villages is 50 kmh (35 mph), 90 kmh (60 mph) on A-roads outside built-up areas and 120 kmh (80 mph) on the motorway. Safety belts (front and back) are compulsory, and children under 12 are not allowed to ride in the front.

3 Car Rental

All the major car hire companies have offices in the main towns, but the most obvious enquiry point is Faro International Airport, the usual pick-up/drop-off point for visitors. To hire a car, you'll need your passport and a full international driving licence.

4 Coach Services

The Algarve is well served by coach and bus companies, with daily connections between a network of coastal and inland towns. Tickets must be pre-booked and can be purchased from main bus stations. Express services have WCs on board and provide video entertainment.

5 Local Bus Services

Cost effective, if slow, local bus services operate well between most coastal towns. Inland, however, the service is infrequent at best. Always put your arm out to flag down an approaching bus, and note that bus stop signs (look out for the word *paragem*) can be placed on the opposite side of the road.

6 Rail Services

CP (Caminhos de Ferro Portuguese) operate a regional train service (no reservation necessary) along the Algarve coast between Vila Real de Santo António and Lagos, with several trains daily in each direction. You have to connect at Tunes for inter-regional and mainline routes heading north (which must be pre-booked).

7 Taxi Services

Taxis use a fixed tariff system, so establish the price before setting off. The minimum flat rate is 2.50 euros, a telephone booking adds 75 centimes, and luggage in the boot adds 1.50 euros. Rates jump up 20 per cent 10pm–6am, on weekends and public holidays. Tipping, around 10 per cent of the total fare, is at your discretion.

8 Helicopters

Almancil-based HTA Helicopters Lda operate a fleet of modern, comfortable helicopters with a maximum range of 700 km (500 miles). They can be hired for business or leisure (aerial photography in particular), and a varying number of destinations throughout Portugal are served, as well as Spain and even North Africa.

9 Boats and Yachts

The River Guadiana is navigable from Vila Real de Santo António up to Alcoutim, and it's also possible to sail along the Arade, though this stretch is really the preserve of sightseeing tour boats. Coastal excursions are popular, and there are several marinas for safely docking yachts.

10 Cycling

In Portugal, cycling is more sport than leisure, which unfortunately means there are few cycle paths. Mountain biking is more popular, and the Algarve hills have some great treks.

Directory

Eva Coaches
Faro • (289) 899 760

Renex Coaches
Faro • (289) 812 980

Train Information
(808) 208 208

HTA Helicopters Lda
(289) 435 112

Left **Tourist brochures** Centre **Newspaper stall** Right **City signs**

TOP 10 General Information

1 Algarve Regional Tourist Board

The RTA head office can supply the addresses and telephone numbers for all regional tourist offices. Their website (www.turismodoalgarve.pt) is currently only in Portuguese, but the RTA's tourist information helpline operates in Portuguese, English, Spanish and French.

2 Internet Sites

Two merit particular mention for their ease of use, the information supplied and the links offered. Browse them at: www.portugal-info.net and www.algarvenet.com.

3 Classifieds

123 Algarve is a weekly newspaper published in English, German and Portuguese featureing hundreds of classifieds, from property to services, and an entertainments supplement.

4 RTA Pamphlets

Algarve Tips is a free monthly pamphlet published on behalf of the RTA. It's a goldmine for information on museums, restaurants and nightclubs, and it is available at most tourist offices. Listings are in English and Portuguese.

5 Tourist Magazines and Newspapers

Essential Algarve is a glossy, bi-monthly publication featuring in-depth articles on spa resorts, golf courses, property, travel and finance. It is published in English and German. *Welcome to the Algarve* is a free English-language monthly newspaper with restaurant reviews, sightseeing tips and useful pull-out city maps. It's available in a host of bars, restaurants and shops.

6 Local Newspapers and Books

An Algarve institution, *The Resident* is a weekly English-language publication packed full of news, views and comment about all things Algarve. *The News* is a national, weekly, English-language newspaper that includes Algarve domestic news. Books on the Algarve written by locals include *Southern Portugal: Its People, Traditions and Wildlife*, which delves into the history and culture of almost every town and village in the southern Alentejo and Algarve.

7 Weather

Spring and autumn are the best times to visit. The winter months are mild – temperatures rarely fall below freezing. July and August can be uncomfortably hot.

8 Opening Hours at Sights

Major museums are usually open 10am–5pm Tuesday to Sunday. Some close for a two-hour lunch break. Major churches are open during the day without a fixed timetable, although some may close between noon and 4pm. Smaller churches and those in rural areas may only be open for services.

9 Public Holidays

The following days are public (bank) holidays in Portugal: 1 January; Carnival Tuesday in February/March (variable), Good Friday, March/April (variable); Revolution Day, 25 April; May Day, 1 May; Corpus Christi, May/June (variable); Camões Day, 10 June; Feast of the Assumption, 15 August; Republic Day, 5 October; All Saints' Day, 1 November; National Independence Day, 1 December; Immaculate Conception, 8 December; Christmas Day, 25 December.

10 Municipal Holidays

In addition to the above, every town celebrates a local (municipal) holiday, affecting opening times and sometimes public transport schedules. Check the local press.

Directory

RTA Head Office
Avenida 5 de Outubro, 18, 8000-076, Faro
• (289) 800 400/424

Tourist Information Free Helpline
800 296 296

Left **Museum, closed on Mondays** Centre **Fresh fish, not on Mondays** Right **Sign for campsite**

Top 10 Things to Avoid

1 August in the Algarve

It's just about impossible to find any accommodation unless booked well in advance, and bars, restaurants and clubs are uncomfortably full. It's also the hottest and driest time of the year.

2 Swimming When a Red Flag is Up

This is an official warning posted by the lifeguard that the water is unsafe, either because of a strong tide, a powerful undertow or (rarely) because of pollution. A green flag fluttering over the sand indicates that conditions are ideal; a yellow flag suggests caution – the tide may be on the turn. Do adhere to these warnings: people have lost their lives in the calmest-looking waters.

3 Drinking and Driving

The maximum legal blood-alcohol level in Portugal is 0.05 per cent (two small beers or a glass of wine). Even then, this figure may well be reviewed to reduce the percentage to just 0.02 per cent, effectively putting you over the limit even after one small beer. Those caught can expect a night in the cells (a weekend if you're pulled over on a Friday), a swift court appearance, a heavy fine and possibly even a jail sentence.

4 Discarding a Lit Cigarette

The entire Algarve is tinder-dry mid-summer and very susceptible to forest fires. Under no account light open fires away from designated barbecue areas; never discard a lit cigarette or match in the countryside.

5 Signing a Time-Share Deal

Refuse point-blank to sign up to any timeshare scheme on the street. If you are interested in purchasing real estate in this manner the best advice you can seek is from someone who has successfully – and happily – already done so and make a note of the property agent involved.

6 The Old 24-hour Currency Exchanges

Until recently, a handy way of obtaining cash out of banking hours was to use a currency exchange machine, similar in operation to an ATM. However, since the introduction of the euro, these devices are largely redundant and susceptible to mechanical failure.

7 Visiting Museums on Mondays

Many museums are closed on Mondays. There are some exceptions, but it's always better to check ahead rather than arrive and be disappointed. The same goes for public holidays, although during the summer these official days off are often ignored in favour of extra business.

8 Conducting Business between 1pm and 3pm

Lunches are long. The Latin notion that it takes two hours to savour a dish of sardines and half a bottle of wine rings true throughout much of the region, especially in rural areas, and particularly on Fridays.

9 Buying Fish on Mondays

Many trawler crews take Sunday night off and only resume work the following evening. This means that some fish offered for sale on Monday mornings might have been caught some 12 hours earlier and refrigerated before ending up in the market.

10 Camping on Beaches

This is strictly a no-go. The Portuguese character is very welcoming and accommodating, but the authorities do not take kindly to flagrant disregard of its countrywide policy banning camping on its beaches. This ruling is particularly upheld along the west coast where there are large expanses of deserted beach. Regular police patrols ensure that miscreants receive a substantial fine if discovered.

Left **Pottery shop** Centre **Fish market** Right **Loulé shopping street**

Top 10 Shopping Tips

1 Visit a Market at the Busiest Time

To get a real flavour of the Algarve's markets, go in the early morning when they are at their busiest. This is when the locals are out bagging the best deals. The fish market at Quarteira (Wednesday mornings) and Loulé's fantastic Saturday market are most vibrant at 9am.

2 Shop Hours

Normal shop hours are 9am–1pm and 3pm–7pm, Mon–Fri. In rural areas most shops close Saturday afternoons and all day Sunday. In the tourist zones, however, many proprietors extend their opening hours throughout the evening.

3 Malls and Hypermarkets

It's easy to spend an entire day in one of the modern shopping malls, such as Forum Algarve (Faro) and Algarve Shopping (Guia). There, large international stores and hypermarkets sell everything under the sun and usually stay open till 10pm. They are also open on Sundays (although some shops within the malls do shut). Cinemas, children's play centres, bars and restaurants are all on hand.

4 Budget Day

If shopping within a budget, steer clear of imported brands, no matter how much they remind you of home. Tinned goods especially are vastly overpriced. In any case, the Portuguese equivalent is generally equal in quality and certainly better value.

5 Taxes – Lighten the Load

There's no more duty-free shopping in Portugal's airports, but non-EU tourists should look out for the Europe Tax-Free Shopping Portugal logo displayed in shops. In some circumstances non-EU citizens are eligible for an IVA (Imposto Sobre Valor Acrescentado), or sales tax refund. Minimum purchase is around €55. The goods, refund cheque and your passport should be presented at Faro customs on departure for a refund by post.

6 Shellfish Shopping

The Algarve is famed for its *marisco* (shellfish), and the choice is bewildering. Open-air markets and supermarkets have shellfish counters where stock is packed in ice or submerged in water to keep it fresh and moist. The best time to shop for seafood, though, is really during the colder months when it's at its tastiest.

7 Finding the Best Pottery

Ceramic and earthenware goods are typical of the Algarve's more traditional wares and make great souvenirs. The small village of Porches, just off the EN125 between Alcantarilha and Lagoa is famed throughout Portugal for its ceramics. Porches Pottery has an outstanding array of cups, mugs, plates, saucers, pots and vases for sale.

8 Roadside Bargains

The Algarve has splendid citrus fruits, especially oranges. Some of the biggest, sweetest and juiciest can be bought from the simple roadside stalls scattered around inland towns and villages, especially near Silves.

9 Catch a Cataplana

The *cataplana* is one of the Algarve's most characteristic copperware goods. It is used for cooking stews and is shaped like a wok, with a snap-down concave lid. The best can be bought in Loulé, notably at Barracha Artesanato, next to the market.

10 Monchique Moonshine

If you're after the best *medronho (aguardiente* – brandy), head for Monchique and seek out the homemade moonshine. This local firewater is made from the berries of the *arbutus*, or strawberry tree. Those in the know say that the best has a yellow tinge to the otherwise clear liquid.

Left **Restaurant menu board** Centre **Café, Lagos** Right **Local wine**

TOP 10 Eating and Drinking Tips

1 Believe Word of Mouth Recommendations

Despite the glossiest of brochures and the slickest of advertising, nothing sells a restaurant menu better than word of mouth. It's the best recommendation you can have, especially if it's from someone you know. Some restaurants trumpet their menu choice without taking too much care about the ingredients. Take time to ask around rather than settling for the nearest. The listings within this guide are the author's recommendations.

2 Order Sardines in Summer

When it comes to sardines, they are best eaten during the summer months. This is when they are firm and at their plumpest. The fish must be charcoal-grilled the same day they are caught to ensure optimum flavour.

3 Consider the Dish of the Day

For a quick, inexpensive meal, simply order the *prato do dia* (dish of the day) from the menu, whatever it happens to be. Locals often ask for the *prato do dia*, and it often proves to be the best choice – invariably wholesome, probably cheaper than the rest of the menu, and served up with little delay.

4 Ask for Half Measures

If you're not too hungry but would still prefer a meal to a snack, ask for a *meia dose* or *mini-prato* (half portion). Most restaurants are happy to oblige. This is also a good option for children.

5 Specify Your Beers

When you ask for *cerveja* (beer) you'll get a lager. To order draft beer, ask for *uma imperial* (small beer) or *uma caneca* (large). If you prefer a bottle, order *uma garrafa de cerveja*. The two top brands are Super Bock and Sagres; the latter also brews *cerveja preta*, the nearest you'll get to a brown ale.

6 Tip the Right Amount

Tipping depends on how much you enjoyed the food and the quality of service. Between 10 per cent and 15 per cent of the total bill is usual.

7 Watch Out for those Extras

The sliced bread, glistening olives and tuna fish paste that land on your table before the meal begins in earnest is listed as *couvert* on the menu. You should decline the offer and send them back if you don't want them. Then check that they haven't been included in the final bill, which occasionally happens as an honest mistake.

8 Look at the Wine Label

The choicest wines are those with the description *reserva a garrafeira* on the label. Expect to pay more for these wines and those of vintage quality.

9 Find a Minimum Smoking Zone

No-smoking areas in Portuguese restaurants are very rare, and lighting up between courses is quite usual. This can be annoying for non-smokers, so it's best to ask for a window seat or, if the weather is fine, choose to sit on the terrace if that is an option. Non-smokers booking by telephone should enquire if there is a no-smoking section of the restaurant.

10 Use the Complaints Book if Necessary

All restaurants have, or should have, a *livro de reclamações* (complaints book). Don't be put off using it if you have a genuine grievance and keep a copy of the entry. If eating in a hotel restaurant the complaints procedure is relatively straightforward. Elsewhere, you may have a harder job, especially in some rural areas. That said, service is generally very good everywhere and there'll be few instances when you have to seek redress.

It's not easy being vegetarian in Portugal; whenever possible, phone a restaurant first to check if they will prepare a vegetarian meal.

Left **Public phone booth** Centre **Post boxes** Right **Post office**

TOP 10 Banking and Communications

1 Banking Hours

Banking hours are 8:30am–3pm Monday to Friday. Monday mornings tend to be busy, so if you have bank business to attend to get there early.

2 Changing Money

Look for the desks marked *câmbios* to change travellers' cheques. Banks charge up to €12.50 commission, exchange bureaux about €5. Travellers' cheques can also be changed at hotels and guesthouses, but check the charges first, as they vary considerably.

3 Money Through the Wall

A far easier way to obtain funds is via an automatic teller machine (ATM). Visa, AmEx, Access/Mastercard or similar can be used to withdraw cash in euros, and most machines have instructions in several languages. Look for the blue *multibanco* sign.

4 Using Credit Cards

Major credit cards are widely accepted in the main towns, but always ask if in doubt and make sure your brand of card is accepted. In rural areas, however, it's best to carry cash.

5 Post Offices

Post offices open weekdays 8.30am–6pm. The branch in Faro, on Largo do Carmo, is also open on Saturday mornings. There are two services: *Correiro normal* and *Correiro azul*. The former is for ordinary post and airmail, and red post boxes should be used for such mail. *Correiro azul* is the priority/express service and uses blue post boxes.

6 Telephone Cards

Telephone cards (*cartão telefónico*) are widely available from post offices, shops and newsagents. The only drawback to the cards is that it is difficult to ascertain how many units you have left.

7 Mobile Phone Hire

You can rent a mobile phone (*telemóvel*) at Faro airport and many other outlets. Look for the Telecel office in the main terminal building. A refundable deposit of €350 is required, and you pay only for calls you make.

8 Directory Enquiries

Dial 118 and the operator will ask you in Portuguese what number you require. Though most operators speak English, ask your hotel for assistance if you don't speak Portuguese.

9 Tuning In

The Algarve has its very own English-language radio station. Tune into Kiss FM (101.2 fm) for news and flight bulletins, weather reports, commercials and some pretty good music.

10 Internet and Email Access

The quickest and easiest way of staying in touch with home is often via email. Boxed here are ten of the best internet cafés in the Algarve.

Internet Cafés

PostNet, Tavira
Rua Dr Silvestre Falcão, Lote 6

Inédita, Albufeira
Travessa dos Telheiros, 2

E-m@ilbox, Lagos
Rua Cândido dos Reis, 112

Club 39 Bar, Armação de Pêra
Rua Dr José António dos Santos

Ciber Espaço, Loulé
Casa da Cultura, Praça da República, 36

Casa dos Condes, Alcoutim
Praça da República

Computa Bar, Carvoeiro
Rua de Escondinho, 8

RB C@fé, Rocha Brava
Loja F, Urbaniz Rocha Brava-Alfanzina

Ciberlusa, Faro
Rua Conselheiro de Bívar, 40

Left **Pharmacy sign** Centre **Sun-lovers** Right **Hospital sign**

TOP 10 Security and Health Matters

1 Calling Emergency Services

To contact the emergency services dial 112 (toll-free). Most operators speak at least two foreign languages, usually including English.

2 Hospitals in the Algarve

There are three main hospitals in the region: Faro district hospital, Portimão and Lagos. All towns have a *centro de saúde* (health centre) that can deal with less serious medical problems.

3 Medical Insurance

Citizens of the EU are entitled to free emergency treatment if they possess an E111 certificate, or equivalent, and a valid passport. Visitors from elsewhere should ensure they have adequate health insurance for emergency medical care and extra cover if they plan to indulge in adventurous sports, such as surfing, diving or horse riding.

4 Pharmacies

In Portugal, *farmácias* (pharmacies) are easily identified by their green cross sign. These are found everywhere in larger towns but are not so abundant in rural communities. Usually very well supplied, many have English-speaking staff and sometimes German, Spanish and French speakers in the resorts. There's always a pharmacy open late; look for the list of late-night services posted on pharmacy windows.

5 Safety on the Beach

Safety flags fly over the beaches throughout the summer and should not be ignored. A green flag means it's safe to swim; a yellow one urges caution and a red flag indicates that it's unsafe to enter the sea.

6 Avoid Sunburn

With near cloudless skies, there's a very real risk of serious sunburn, so be sure to use a sunscreen lotion that's strong enough for your skin type. The sun is fiercest between noon and 3pm, when it's best to seek out a parasol or shady beachfront café.

7 Don't Dehydrate

Drink plenty of water! Tap water is safe. There's also a vast choice of bottled mineral water – *com gaz* (fizzy) and *naturale* (still). In midsummer, aim to drink around two litres a day.

8 Precautions Against Theft

Petty theft is increasingly common in the Algarve, so take a few sensible precautions, such as not flaunting expensive watches and cameras, and never leaving valuables unattended. Avoid leaving personal items in the car, even in the boot – hire cars are easily recognized by would-be thieves.

9 Identification

Always carry some means of identification with you and have car documents to hand when driving. Failure to produce identification if stopped by the police may result in a hefty fine, even if you are blameless in all other respects.

10 Loss of Passport

Report such a loss to the police immediately. You should also inform your embassy or consulate. To facilitate enquiries, make copies of all important documents and leave them in your room safe or another secure place.

Directory of Hospitals

Faro District Hospital
Rua Leão Penedo
• (289) 802 444; (289) 802 555

Portimão Hospital
Sítio do Poço Seco
• (282) 450 300

Lagos Hospital
Rua Castelo dos Governadores
• (282) 770 100

Left **Camping, Albufeira** Right **Public transport**

Top 10 Ways to Save Money

1 Visit in Low Season

For some spectacular bargains, visit in January and February. Although many places are closed for the winter, prices for accommodation can be as much as 50 per cent less than in peak season.

2 Take a Tent

This is the cheapest option in the Algarve, but you must use official campsites. There are dozens of these along the coast and quite a few inland. Prices do rise during the high season, but you can still expect to pay only around €5 per adult per night for a small tent. Unfortunately, many campsites close in low season.

3 Stay in Youth Hostels

If you're eligible, staying in youth hostels is another inexpensive option, although there are no single room rates and prices can creep up in the summer. There are five hostels in the Algarve: Alcoutim, Vila Real de Santo António, Faro, Portimão and Lagos. If you don't already have a Hostelling International card from your national hostel association you can obtain a "guest card". Advance booking is essential in summer.

4 Rent a Quarto

Local tourist offices can sometimes provide a list of homeowners renting out *quartos* (private rooms), with shared facilities, at very reasonable rates. It is also possible to rent the occasional beach hut on a strictly temporary basis. Again, the tourist office may be able to help. Otherwise look out for *quarto* signs in windows, on notice boards etc.

5 Get a Youth Discount Card

Popular youth-card schemes such as Euro<26 and Go25/IYTC allow card holders good discounts on a wide range of attractions and services, including travel, museum and cinema tickets.

6 Get a Senior Rail Card

Senior citizens aged 65 and over heading for the Algarve are eligible for a 50 per cent discount on weekday rail travel using the *cartão dourado* (senior card), which can be purchased at ticket counters. Note that discounted tickets can only be purchased at certain main-line stations and cannot be used on suburban commuter trains at rush hour.

7 Eat with Locals

Whenever possible, eat where the locals eat. It may be no more than a 'hole-in-the-wall' taverna, and the fare may be presented without finesse, but the food will be much cheaper than opting for a beachfront restaurant. The *prato do dia* (dish of the day) is usually the cheapest on the menu.

8 Use Public Transport Instead of Hitch-hiking

While hitch-hiking may cost next to nothing, it's not recommended in Portugal. The Portuguese have an ambivalent attitude towards hitch-hikers. You may catch a lift within minutes or you may stay all day on the same spot. It's much easier to use the cheap and efficient public transport. Another more sobering reason not to try and hitch-hike is the appalling road safety record held by Portuguese drivers.

9 Return Your Empties

Stocking up on empty beer bottles? If they're Sagres or Super Bock take the empties back to the local supermarket (not the big hypermarkets) for a discount against your next "round" of the same brand.

10 Buy the Cheapest Cinema Tickets

On Mondays, cinemas across Portugal offer discounted seats, but be prepared to queue, especially if you want to see the latest Hollywood blockbuster. Foreign films are never dubbed but subtitled instead.

Left **Balaia Golf** Centre **Disabled sign** Right **Room phone**

Top 10 Accommodation Tips

1 Book Online
Where possible, consider booking upmarket hotels online or through a travel agent. At many places you'll get a cheaper rate. Portugal Hotel Guide has an online booking link, as does the Portugal Travel Guide.

2 Haggle Over Room Rates
Room rates plummet out of season but it's still worth haggling over a price to determine the bottom line. This is especially so if you're a family or a small group. After all, no hotel likes empty beds. You may also be able to conjure up a deal if you decide you want to stay longer than originally planned. Try and negotiate a "package" if the hotel isn't expecting to fill up.

3 Share the Room with Your Children
Children under the age of eight are entitled to 50 per cent discount in many hotels and guesthouses if they share their parents' room. Enquire about this possibility before checking in. It's also a good idea to see the room before accepting it.

4 Time Your Golfing Holiday
Remember that if considering a golfing holiday in the Algarve, the main season is from November to March and early April. The region's golf courses get very busy in December and again in late January, February and March. The hotels linked with golf courses offer their guests preferential green fee rates, which can save the dedicated golfer a considerable amount.

5 Seek Out Disabled Facilities
Wheeling Around the Algarve is an organization that sources suitable accommodation for people in wheelchairs. It also points out disabled-friendly restaurants and car-hire companies. The organization is run by David Player, himself a wheelchair user, and he personally inspects all properties recommended.

6 Look into Long-Term Packages
Throughout the low season it's possible to rent accommodation on a long-term basis – anything up to six months. Apartments in villa complexes are a good option, as they tend to be bereft of life outside the summer season. The swimming pool may not be full, but the atmosphere will be peaceful. The best line of enquiry is through the tourism office nearest to your desired location.

7 Bring an Adapter
Electricity is 220V, 50Hz, and plugs normally have two round pins. So bring an adapter for shavers, hairdryers etc.

8 Pack an Insect Repellent
Rooms in rural hotels invariably attract annoying flying bugs, especially mosquitoes. It's a good idea to pack a slow-burning insect repellent coil and let it smoke for an hour or so before retiring to bed.

9 Avoid Using the Room Phone
Direct-dial hotel telephone charges in Portugal are extortionate compared to those in the rest of Europe. Avoid them unless absolutely necessary.

10 Use the Hotel Fax Machine
In contrast to phoning from your room, prices for faxing from *pensões* and *residenciais* are considerably lower than using the post office where the rates are unreasonably high.

Directory

Online Booking
www.hotelguide.pt
www.portugaltravel guide.com

Orbitur
Lisbon • (218) 117 000

Wheeling Around the Algarve
Rua 5 de Outubro 181, Apartado 3421, Almansil • (289) 393 636 • www.player.pt

Left **Sheraton Algarve** Centre **Le Meridien Penina** Right **Vila Vita Parc**

Top 10 Luxury, Five-Star Hotels

1 Hotel Quinta do Lago

Overlooking Ria Formosa lagoon and the ocean, this sophisticated resort has two great restaurants, the Brisa do Mar (traditional Portuguese cuisine) and Cá d'Oro (famed for its Venetian gastronomy). Leisure facilities include golf and a health club with gym, sauna and massage. *Quinta do Lago, Almansil • Map J5 • (289) 350 350 • www.quintadolagohotel.com • €€€€€*

2 Vila Vita Parc

An exclusive clifftop estate set in lush sub-tropical gardens reflecting Moorish-style architecture. Accommodation is either in the main hotel or in sumptuous villa suites. Leisure facilities include golf, in- and outdoor pools, tennis courts and one of Portugal's best natural therapy centres. *Alporchinhos, Porches, Armação de Pêra • Map F5 • (282) 310 100 • www.vilavitaparc.com • €€€€€*

3 Le Meridien Penina Golf & Resort

Surrounded by verdant woodland, the Penina has an 18-hole championship golf course *(see p46)* and a further two nine-hole courses. Four restaurants, horse riding, water sports and a health centre complete the package. *8501-952 Portimão • Map E5 • (282) 420 200 • www.lemeridien-penina.com • €€€€*

4 Sofitel Vilalara Thalassa

Vilalara features one of the world's finest thalassotherapy (sea-water bathing) centres and an extensive range of facilities and treatments for health, beauty and wellbeing. An excellent restaurant is also on hand. *Praia das Gaivotas, Porches, Lagoa • Map E4 • (282) 320 000 • www.sofitel.com • €€€€€*

5 Le Meridien Dona Filipa

Situated in the grounds of the exclusive Vale do Lobo resort, the Dona Filipa is well-situated for the Royal golf course, Ocean course and the San Lorenzo. A first-class tennis academy is also close by. *Vale do Lobo, Almansil • Map J5 • (289) 357 200 • www.lemeridien-donafilipa.com • €€€€€*

6 Sheraton Algarve Hotel & Resort

Perched above some of the Algarve's best beaches, special features include a childrens' entertainment village and a 9-hole golf course. All rooms have sun terraces, and guests have access to a private beach club. *Praia da Falésia, Albufeira • Map G5 • (289) 500 100 • www.luxurycollection.com • €€€€€*

7 Pestana Carlton Alvor Hotel

A modern hotel nestling in manicured gardens and ideally situated for golfers, with preferential green fees available for a number of golf courses including Pestana's own. *Praia dos Três Irmãos, Alvor • Map D4 • (282) 400 900 • www.pestana.com • €€€€*

8 Tivoli Marinotel

Set right on the beach, so every bedroom balcony has stunning views of either the sea or the marina. A range of water sports are close at hand, and the Sirius Grill, with its panoramic vista, is ideal for formal dining. *Vilamoura marina • Map H5 • (289) 303 303 • www.tivolihotels.com • €€€€€*

9 Hotel Atlantis Vilamoura

Ideal for families, the Atlantis has sports and leisure facilities in abundance, including a "Children's Zone", four swimming pools and several restaurants. *Rua do Oceano Atlântico, Vilamoura • Map H5 • (289) 381 600 • www.graopara.pt • €€€€*

10 Hotel Algarve Casino

Glowing in its beachfront location in Praia da Rocha, this was Portugal's first hotel-casino complex. The casino, with its superb gaming rooms and international cabaret, remains the prize draw. *Avenida Tomás Cabreira, Praia da Rocha • Map E5 • (282) 402 000 • www.solverde.pt • €€€€*

***Note:** Unless otherwise stated, all hotels accept credit cards, have en-suite bathrooms and air conditioning*

Left **Bela Vista** Right **Tivoli Almansor**

Price Categories

For a standard, double room per night (with breakfast if included), taxes and extra charges.	€ under €50
	€€ €50–€100
	€€€ €100–€200
	€€€€ €200–€300
	€€€€€ over €300

TOP 10 Four-Star Hotels

1 Estalagem Vila Joya

This gourmet retreat is set amidst splendid seafront gardens and is home to Portugal's only two-star Michelin restaurant (open to non-residents). Rooms and suites are individually decorated but are only available on a half-board basis (breakfast and evening meal). ⓢ *Praia da Galé, Albufeira • Map G5 • (289) 591 836 • vila.joya@clix.pt • No credit cards • Closed Nov–Mar • €€€€€*

2 Tivoli Almansor

Commanding views over precipitous cliffs, this hotel is within easy walking distance of Carvoeiro town centre. The interior decoration is Moorish in influence and rooms have spectacular ocean vistas. The health club has Jacuzzi, sauna and Turkish bath, and there is a diving school near the bay. ⓢ *Vale Covo, Apartado 1299, Carvoeiro • Map E5 • (282) 351 100 • www.tivolihotels.com • €€€*

3 Hotel Vila Galé Albacora

Converted from former fishermen's houses, the hotel has a chapel and museum incorporated into its structure. Most rooms have views of the Ria Formosa. Courtesy boat transport is offered to nearby Tavira island. ⓢ *Apartado 2, Quatro Águas, Tavira • Map M4 • (281) 380 800 • €€€€*

4 Estalagem Abrigo da Montanha

This granite, mountain inn is set in terraced gardens bursting with a fine collection of camellias. The views are spectacular, especially from the side of the pool. ⓢ *Corte Pereira Estrada da Fóia, Monchique • Map E3 • (282) 912 131 • abrigodamontanha@hotmail.com • €€*

5 Bela Vista

A charming example of an early 20th-century Algarve guest house, Bela Vista's interior glows with beautiful azulejos panels. Situated right on Praia da Rocha, this is a wonderful alternative to the modern aparthotels and villas. ⓢ *Avenida Tómas Cabreira, Praia da Rocha • Map E5 • (282) 450 480 • www.hotelbelavista.net • €€€*

6 Pousada de São Brás

The yellow shutters of this hotel sparkle over the quiet town of São Brás de Alportel. Most rooms overlook a hinterland of olive and cork trees, while the pool, tennis facilities and regional cuisine completes the picture. ⓢ *Pousada de São Brás, Poço dos Ferreiros, São Brás de Alportel • Map K4 • (289) 842 305/6 • www.pousadas.pt • €€€*

7 Estalagem do Guadiana

Unrivalled as the best hotel along the Guadiana, guests here wake up to a view of the river and rural Spain beyond. An ideal place to relax and unwind. ⓢ *Estalagem do Guadiana, Alcoutim • Map P1 • (281) 540 120 • €€€*

8 Hotel Tivoli Lagos

Near the old town, this smart hotel consists of a series of buildings linked around a swimming pool. Guests also have the use of an exclusive beach club down on the seafront. ⓢ *Rua Nova da Aldeia, Lagos • Map D5 • (282) 790 079 • €€€*

9 Hotel Eva

Very comfortable and conveniently situated right on Faro's marina, the panorama from the rooftop swimming pool is outstanding and takes in the Ria Formosa and the surrounding lagoons. The city's historic old quarter is a five-minute walk away. ⓢ *Avenida da República, 1, Faro • Map K6 • (289) 803 354 • €€€*

10 Albergaria Vila Lido

Jacqueline Kennedy was a guest here in the days when this immaculately kept inn was a private villa. Located near the fort and dating from the 19th century, the period detail is exquisite. Light floods the verandah in late afternoon, and tea on the terrace comes with a fabulous sea view. ⓢ *Avenida Tómas Cabreira, Praia da Rocha • Map E5 • (282) 424 127 • €€*

Left **Hotel Guadiana** Right **Hotel Colina dos Mouras**

TOP 10 Three-Star Hotels

1 Aqua Meia Praia

The striking blue-and-white façade is hard to miss, and the stylish interior design is equally ebullient. Embroidered gardens of palm and pine surround an inviting pool, although the huge Meia Praia beach is just five minutes away. *Meia Praia, Lagos • Map D5 • (282) 762 001 • www.hotelaquameiapraia.com • €€€*

2 Hotel Guadiana

This refurbished 19th-century property is a classified national monument and its grand façade and grace evoke a less hurried era. However, the elegant interior and period architecture belies the hotel's modern infrastructure. The front rooms command glorious views across the River Guadiana. *Avenida da República, 94-96, Vila Real de Santo António • Map P4 • (281) 511 482 • €€*

3 Alte Hotel

Alte is one of the prettiest villages in the Algarve, surrounded as it is by the Serra do Caldeirão mountains. The views from the hotel are stunning although its position at the summit of a hill means that having your own transport is useful. Leisure activities include a swimming pool, tennis court and billiards. *Estrada de Sta. Margarida, Montinho-Alte, Loulé • Map J4 • (289) 478 524 • www.altehotel.com • €€*

4 Hotel Colina dos Mouras

A cracking view of Silves castle is to be had from the back rooms of this friendly hotel, just a few minutes' walk from the town's historic quarter. A sun terrace overlooks a circular pool and rows of orange groves. *Pocinho Santo, Silves • Map F4 • (282) 440 420 • €€*

5 Loulé Jardim

Refurbished to an early 20th-century design, the beige-and-cream façade faces a quiet park in the centre of Loulé. The town's castle and Saturday market are both within easy reach, and the rooftop pool is a bonus. *Praça Manuel de Arriaga, 8100 Loulé • Map J4 • (289) 413 094/5 • www.loulejardimhotel.com • €€*

6 Hotel da Baleeira

Overlooking the bay, this is an ideal base from which to explore the Sagres promontory and Cabo de São Vicente. The gardens incorporate a pool and lead directly to the beach. *Baleeira, Vila de Sagres • Map B5 • (282) 624 212 • www.sagres.net/sagres/baleeira • No air conditioning • €€*

7 Hotel Califórnia

Within Albufeira's lively bar district, this is the ideal place if heady nightlife is your bag. All bedrooms have terrace views over the town, and Praia dos Barcos is a 10-minute stroll away, though the rooftop pool is just as blissful. *Rua Cândido dos Reis, 12, Albufeira • Map G5 • (289) 583 400 • €€*

8 Hotel Residencial Salema

The hotel building is the centrepiece of an old quay that retains the charm of colourful boats and rows of fishermen's huts. The rooms have great views of the bay, and a number of bars, cafés and restaurants are all within easy reach. *Salema, Vila do Bispo • Map C5 • (282) 695 328 • €€*

9 Hotel Riomar

The majority of rooms have balconies, some with a lovely ocean view, but the hotel's draw is its central position, in the heart of Lagos. The major historical attractions are less than a 10-minute walk away, as are the shops and some great restaurants. *Rua Cândido dos Reis, 83, Lagos • Map D5 • (282) 770 130 • AmEx only • €€*

10 Hotel Dom Bernado

The front rooms of this tidy hotel overlook the Ermida Nossa Senhora da Esperança; top floors command city centre views. Convenient for Faro's main attractions. *Rua General Teófilo da Trindade, 20, Faro • Map K6 • (289) 889 800 • www.hoteldombernado.cjb.net • €€*

***Note:** Unless otherwise stated, all hotels accept credit cards, have en-suite bathrooms and air conditioning*

Left **Residencial Pensão Limas** Centre **Residencial Ponte Romana** Right **Matos Pereira**

Price Categories

For a standard, double room per night (with breakfast if included), taxes and extra charges.

€	under €50
€€	€50–€100
€€€	€100–€200
€€€€	€200–€300
€€€€€	over €300

TOP 10 Pensões and Residencias

1 Residencial Ponte Romana

Standing by the Roman bridge on the south side of the River Arade, this location is hard to beat. The riverside rooms face the castle, and the evening view alone is worth the stay. The restaurant serves generous portions of delicious country cuisine. ✆ *Ponte Romana, Silves • Map F4 • (282) 443 275 • €*

2 Residencial Miradoura da Serra

The hotel name means "mountain viewpoint" and the panorama from this hilltop hideaway doesn't disappoint. Excellent value and a great base for hill walking or pottering about the pleasant market town. All rooms have balcony views. ✆ *Rua Combatentes do Ultramar, Monchique • Map E3 • (282) 912 163 • No credit cards • No air conditioning • €*

3 Pensão Boémia

From its backstreet locations, the light and airy Boémia exudes bonhomie. The top-floor rooms have balconies with views across the town's maze of whitewashed homes. A simple interior and a very steep staircase. ✆ *Rua da Cerca, 20, Olhão • Map L5 • (289) 714 513 • €*

4 Residencial Pensão Limas

Wedged between bars and restaurants in a narrow, pedestrianized thoroughfare, Limas' bright yellow sun blinds grace a whitewashed façade. The staircase inside is steep and narrow, and leads to modest, functional bedrooms. ✆ *Rua da Liberdade, 25–27, Albufeira • Map G5 • (289) 514 025 • No Credit Cards • €*

5 Casa Sagres

Ivy-clad walls surround a sun-trap patio, which forms part of the dining facility at this breezy, stone and whitewash building. The clipped garden overlooks the Atlantic, as do some of the rooms of this popular hotel. ✆ *Praça da República, Sagres • Map B6 • (282) 624 358 • No air conditioning • €€*

6 Residencial Lagôas Bica

Polished black and white azulejos decorate the façade of this well-known pensão. Its proximity to the historic centre of Tavira makes it very popular in summer, so phone ahead to check room availability. ✆ *Rua Almirante Cândido dos Reis, 24, Tavira • Map M4 • (281) 322 252 • No credit cards • No air conditioning • €*

7 Pensão Residencial Oceano

A mere stone's throw from Faro's historical quarter, this pensão in the shape of a traditional town house is also handy for shops, restaurants, cafés and the local tourism office. ✆ *Travessa Ivens, 21, Faro • Map K6 • (289) 823 349 • No air conditioning • €*

8 Pensão Luar

Some of the rooms here overlook the sweeping River Seixe valley, and this friendly *pensão* is ideal for the beach at Odeceixe. While secluded, this area is popular in summer so booking is advisable. ✆ *Rua da Vázea, 28, Odeceixe • Map C1 • (282) 947 194 • No credit cards • No air conditioning • €*

9 Residência Matos Pereira

Set in a pedestrianized street, the Residência looks like a typical town house, matched by an atmosphere that is both domestic and jovial. ✆ *Rua Dr Sousa Martins, 57, Vila Real de Santo António • Map P4 • (281) 543 325 • No credit cards • No air conditioning • €*

10 Pensão Residencial Avenida Nova

The pale pink façade of this solid building stands smartly over Avenida 25 de Abril and the Rua Maria Campina. Some rooms are large and therefore handy for families. ✆ *Rua Maria Campina, 1, Loulé • Map J4 • (289) 415 097 • No credit cards • Only two rooms with en-suite bathroom • No air conditioning • €*

Left **Le Meridien Penina** Centre **Hotel Quinta Do Lago** Right **Vila Vita Parc**

Top 10 Hotels with Golf Courses

1 Le Meridien Penina Golf & Resort

Guests of this five-star resort have the privileged use of the 18-hole Championship layout *(see p46)*, which has hosted the Portuguese Open several times. There are a couple of 9-hole courses too *(see p48)*. *Penina 8501-952 Portimão • Map E4 • (282) 420 200 • www.lemeridienpenina.com • €€€€*

2 Sheraton Algarve Hotel & Resort

The 18th hole of the hotel's spectacular clifftop course is known as the "Devil's Parlour": a long shot from the tee must carry over a deep chasm in order to reach the final green. The course and luxury hotel form the hub of the exclusive Pine Cliffs resort. *Praia da Falésia, Albufeira • Map G5 • (289) 500 100 • www.luxurycollection.com • €€€€€*

3 Hotel Quinta do Lago

The hotel is within one of the most luxurious golfing resorts in Europe. It encompasses no fewer than three championship courses, including the par 72 Quinta do Lago. Six more layouts are within easy reach. The hotel offers special golf tuition packages and there are special green fee rates for guests. *Quinta do Lago, Almansil • Map J5 • (289) 350 350 • www.quintadolagohotel.com • €€€€€*

4 Le Meridien Dona Filipa

This five-star hotel owns the magnificent San Lorenzo course. Priority of play at this par 72 scenic masterpiece is given to hotel guests. *Vale do Lobo, Almansil • Map J5 • (289) 357 200 • www.lemeridien-donafilipa.com • €€€€€*

5 Pestana Carlton Alvor Hotel

An ideal five-star base for golfers, with generous discounts offered at a dozen nearby courses, including Pestana's Pinta and Gramacho layouts at Carvoeiro, home of the David Leadbetter Golf Academy. The hotel overlooks Três Irmãos beach and is close to the fishing village of Alvor. *Praia dos Três Irmãos, Alvor • Map D4 • (282) 400 900 • www.pestana.com • €€€€*

6 Tivoli Marinotel

A luxurious five-star hotel near the beach and marina. A free shuttle service operates to the Vilamoura courses Pinhal, Laguna, Millennium, Vila Sol and Old Course. *Vilamoura marina • Map H5 • (289) 303 303 • www.tivolihotels.com • €€€€€*

7 Tivoli Almansor

A spectacular clifftop location, with staff on hand to arrange play at over a dozen courses, all at generous discounts. Almansor owns the 18-hole Salgados layout, which has no fewer than 14 water hazards. *Vale Covo, Apartado 1299, Carvoeiro • Map E5 • (282) 351 100 • www.tivolihotels.com • €€€*

8 Hotel Dom Pedro Golf

This plush, modern hotel is a favourite with Algarve golfers. It has instigated a popular annual amateur golf tournament (Dec/Jan) at the Vila Sol, Pinheiros Altos, Millennium, Old Course and Ria Formosa layouts. Dom Pedro's golf department can also arrange special golf clinics. *Rua Atlântico, Quarteira, Vilamoura • Map H5 • (289) 300 780 • www.dompedro.com • €€€€€*

9 Vila Vita Parc

A luxury resort with its own 9-hole course within the grounds, as well as a driving range and practice green. Tuition can also be arranged, with access to 20 of the Algarve's best courses. *Alporchinhos, Porches, Armação de Pêra • Map F5 • (282) 310 100 • www.vilavitaparc.com • €€€€€*

10 Vila Galé Golfe

Right by Praia da Galé, this modern four-star hotel offers many packages for the serious amateur. Play takes place over several layouts with a free shuttle service. *Praia da Galé, Apartado 108, Albufeira • Map G5 • (289) 570 800 • www.vilagale.pt • €€€€*

Note: Unless otherwise stated, all hotels accept credit cards, have en-suite bathrooms and air conditioning

Left **Belavista da Luz** Right **Dom Pedro Marina**

Price Categories

For a standard, double room per night (with breakfast if included), taxes and extra charges.

€	under €50
€€	€50–€100
€€€	€100–€200
€€€€	€200–€300
€€€€€	over €300

Top 10 Resort Hotels for Families

1 Hotel da Aldeia

Situated in the centre of Albufeira's lively Areias de São João tourism complex. Sweeping terraces overlook verdant gardens, two swimming pools, a tennis court and a children's playground. ⊗ *Avenida Dr Sá Carneiro, Areias de São João, Albufeira • Map G5 • (289) 588 861 • www.maisturismo.pt/haldeia • Babysitting available • €€€*

2 Alvor Atlantic

Attractive aparthotel and villa complex. Its facilities include indoor and outdoor pools, a sauna, gym and supermarket. An imaginative children's park is complemented by nearby golf, tennis and water sports facilities. ⊗ *Praia de Alvor • Map D5 • (282) 400 000 • www.pestana.com • €€€*

3 Hotel Algarve Casino

The complete family holiday package. As well as the famous beach, leisure facilities on hand include a swimming pool, video room, a children's zone and a casino that stages international cabaret. ⊗ *Avenida Tomás Cabreira, Praia da Rocha • Map E5 • (282) 402 000 • www.solverde.pt • Babysitting available • €€€€€*

4 Hotel Casabela

Views across the mouth of the River Arade and close proximity to the pretty fishing village of Ferragudo form a big part of Casabela's appeal. Two swimming pools, one specially adapted for children, a tennis court and pleasant gardens complete the draw. ⊗ *Vale da Areia, Ferragudo • Map E5 • (282) 461 580 • www.hotel-casabela.de • €€€*

5 Hotel Belavista da Luz

A family-run hotel, built in a horseshoe shape to enclose two inviting pools and a "children's zone". Golf, horse riding, walking tours and scuba diving can be organized by staff. ⊗ *Praia da Luz, Lagos • Map D5 • (282) 788 655 • www.belavistadaluz.com • Babysitting available • €€€*

6 Vila Galé Albacora

A buzzing children's club and packed schedule of entertainments keep guests fully occupied. Two swimming pools, a separate children's pool and nearby beaches at Ilha de Tavira make it ideal for water lovers. ⊗ *Quatro Águas, Tavira • Map M4 • (281) 380 800 • Babysitting available • €€€€*

7 Hotel Garbe

Enjoying a prime position on one of the Algarve's most popular beaches, the facilities here include an outdoor pool, games room and hair salon. Evening entertainment takes place in the bar "Boa Vista". ⊗ *Avenida Beira Mar, Apartado 1, Armação de Pêra • Map F5 • (282) 315 187 • Babysitting available • €€€€*

8 Dom Joao II

Overlooking a pristine beach, trim gardens and an outdoor seawater pool, Dom Joao II provides ideal conditions for the perfect family holiday. There's also a "Kids' Club" for both play and learning. ⊗ *Praia de Alvor • Map D5 • (282) 400 700 • www.pestana.com • Babysitting available • €€€€*

9 Hotel Dom Pedro Marina

With its own private beach next to Vilamoura marina and a central location, this is a very popular choice. Facilities include outdoor pools and a restaurant that specializes in fine Italian cuisine. ⊗ *Rua Tivoli, Lote H4, 8125-410 Vilamoura • Map H5 • (289) 381 000 • www.dompedro-hotels.com • Babysitting available • €€€€*

10 Hotel Montechoro

Set within an exciting leisure zone that includes tennis courts, football pitches and swimming pools, this is a perfect choice for active families. Albufeira's stunning beaches provide daytime amusement while many bars provide evening music. ⊗ *Rua Alexandre O'Neil, Montechoro, Albufeira • Map G5 • (289) 589 423 • www.maisturismo.pt/hmontech • Babysitting available • €€€*

Left **Convento de Santo António** Centre **Quinta do Caracol** Right **Monte do Casal**

TOP 10 Unusual Places to Stay

1 Convento de Santo António

Built by Capuchin monks in the 17th century, the six double rooms and one suite in this hallowed building are set around a sunny cloister. Brushed terracotta and patterned azulejos decorate the interior, and breakfast is served to Gregorian chant. Minimum stay applies. *Rua de Santo António, 56, Tavira • Map M4 • (281) 325 632 • American Express only • Air conditioning in selected rooms • €€€*

2 Fortaleza do Beliche

The sturdy, windblown walls of this tiny fortress house just four rooms, which peer across a manicured courtyard and a small chapel. The ocean views across the lawn are magnificent, but to stay you'll need to book several months in advance. *Cabo de São Vicente-Sagres, Vila do Bispo • Map B5 • (282) 624 124 • €€*

3 Monte do Casal

Delightfully secluded in the countryside near Estói, the suites of this converted farmhouse overlook gardens of bougainvillea and swaying palms. The proprietor/chef trained at London's Claridges and Savoy hotels, and the menu is a hallmark of this special retreat. *Cerro do Lobo, 8000-661 Estói • Map K5 • (289) 991 503 • €€€*

4 Quinta do Caracol

A 17th-century farm lovingly converted into a series of beautiful apartments named after flowers. Birdsong from the garden aviary drifts over the shaded, outdoor dining areas. *Rua São Pedro, Tavira • Map M4 • (281) 322 475 • www.quintadocaracol.pa-net.pt • €€€*

5 Casa Domilú

The honeymoon suite, with its sunken whirlpool bath and opulent décor, epitomizes Casa Domilú's ethos of sophistication. Elsewhere, huge bay windows reflect emerald swimming pools, and a luxurious spa is on hand to pamper you. *Estrada de Benagil, Alfanzina, Carvoeiro • Map E5 • (282) 350 610 • www.casa-domilu.com • €€*

6 Albergaria Bica Boa

Wooden floors and ceilings impart a rustic feel to this mountain inn, perched on the lip of a valley, a few minutes' walk out of Monchique. Just four guest rooms and some fine vegetarian food. *Estrada de Sabóia – N266, 8550 Monchique • Map E3 • (282) 912 271 • No air conditioning • €*

7 Quinta das Barradas

Roaming cattle surround the track that leads up to this attractive estate of converted barns and outhouses. Perfect for those seeking privacy, rural air and rustic food. *Odiáxere, 8600 Lagos • Map D5 • (282) 770 200 • No Credit Cards • No air conditioning • €*

8 Quinta do Rio

Orange groves envelope this restored farmhouse, lacing the air here with a tangy aroma. The warm interior retains original wooden beams and traditional furnishings. *Sítio São Estevão, Apartado 217, Silves • Map F4 • (282) 445 528 • No air conditioning • €*

9 Casa da Palmeirinha

This old and graceful Portuguese town house with terracotta floors and *azulejos* panels creates a Mediterranean feel inside. A flourishing roof garden looks over a central patio and modest swimming pool. *Rua da Igreja, 1, Mexilhoeira Grande, Portimão • Map E4 • (282) 969 277 • No credit cards • No air conditioning • €€*

10 Monte Rosa

A splendid old farm complex nestling in the heart of the countryside. An informal atmosphere pervades the rooms and apartments. Dinner can be arranged, and there's a minimum two-day stay. (Camping also available.) *Lagoa da Rosa, Barão de São João • Map C4 • (282) 687 002 • www.monterosaportugal.com • No credit cards • No air con • €*

***Note:** Unless otherwise stated, all hotels accept credit cards, have en-suite bathrooms and air conditioning*

Price Categories

For a standard, double room per night (with breakfast if included), taxes and extra charges.

€	under €50
€€	€50–€100
€€€	€100–€200
€€€€	€200–€300
€€€€€	over €300

Left **Albufeira Camping** Right **Parque de Campismo São Miguel**

TOP 10 Campsites

1 Quinta dos Carriços

Set in a pretty valley, this site offers all necessary facilities – toilets, hot showers, laundry rooms, shops and restaurant. There are studios and apartments for rent too, and there's even a separate area for naturists! *Parque de Campismo, Quinta dos Carriços, Praia da Salema, Budens • Map C5 • (282) 695 201• €*

2 Camping Olhão

This excellent site near the Parque Natural da Ria Formosa has first-class amenities and lively recreation facilities that include a swimming pool and tennis court. There's also a mini-market, a restaurant and a bar. *Pinheiros de Marim, Apartado 300, Olhão • Map L5 • (289) 700 300 • www.sbsi.pt/camping • €*

3 Albufeira Camping

A sprawling camping and caravan site about 2 km (1 mile) from the town centre. Facilities include three pools, an adventure playground, an à la carte restaurant, a supermarket and a night club. *Estrada de Ferreiras, Albufeira • Map G5 • (289) 587 629 • €*

4 Parque de Campismo São Miguel

Secluded under a canopy of pine, this is one of the most modern and comprehensive sites in southern Portugal. Leisure attractions include tennis courts, a swimming pool and a restaurant, and the surrounding countryside is a national park. Caravans and bungalows can also be hired. *São Miguel, Odemira • (282) 947 145 • €*

5 Parque de Campismo Ilha de Tavira

Only tents go up on this island, which is free from cars and caravans. There are supermarket and restaurant facilities, and tent hire is possible too. Access is via ferry at Quatro Águas. The site's hugely popular in summer, so call ahead and ask about special promotions. *Ilha de Tavira • Map M5 • (281) 324 455 • No Credit Cards • €*

6 Parque de Campismo Sagres

It's not uncommon to see surfboards outside the tents here as the site's in easy reach of some of the west coast's finest surfing beaches. Amenities are excellent, and Sagres town is 2 km (1 mile) away. *Cerro das Moitas, Vila do Bispo • Map B5 • (282) 624 371 • www.orbitur.pt • €*

7 Parque de Campismo de Armação de Pêra

The nearest campsite to Armação de Pêra, this is great for anyone holidaying on a budget who craves the sights and nightlife of a lively resort. Modern facilities abound on site, and it's also possible to hire bungalows here. *8365-184 Armação de Pêra • Map F5 • (282) 312 260 • www.roteiro-campista.pt • €*

8 Parque de Campismo Municipal de Monte Gordo

The conifer woodland near the site is home to the largest population of Mediterranean chameleon in Portugal. Walks here are superb, and Monte Gordo itself is a thriving little town with an ideal beach for sunbathing and swimming. *Monte Gordo • Map P4 • (281) 510 970 • €*

9 Camping-Caravaning Vale da Telha

This is located near some incredible beaches, such as Praia de Monte Clérigo – a surfer's gem. Simple amenities include hot showers and a swimming pool. *Praia de Monte Clérigo, Apartado 141, Vale da Telha, Aljezur • Map C2 • (282) 998 444 • €*

10 Camping Dourada

This pleasant and rather tranquil site fills up quickly in summer due to its proximity to the buzzing resort of Alvor. Modern, well-equipped facilities. *EN 531, Alvor • Map D4 • (282) 459 178 • www.roteiro-campista.pt • €*

Left **Hostel sign** Centre **Alcoutim youth hostel** Right **Évora youth hostel**

Top 10 Hostels

1 Pousada da Juventude Lagos
Slap bang in one of the Algarve's best-known resorts, this youth hostel is popular year-round. Airy rooms and dorms surround a courtyard studded with dwarf palms. *Rua Lançarote de Freitas, 50, Lagos • Map D5 • (282) 761 970 • lagos@movijovem.pt • No air conditioning • €*

2 Pousada da Juventude Évora (Alentejo)
Overlooking a tidy square near the town's historic quarter, the terrace views can be inspiring. Facilities here include a games room and internet access. *Rua Miguel Bombarda 40, Évora • (266) 744 848 • evora@movijovem.pt • Air conditioning only in double rooms • €*

3 Pousada da Juventude Alcoutim
This out-of-the-way hostel overlooks River Guadiana, where it's possible to go on canoeing expeditions. There's also a swimming pool, bike rental, table tennis and snooker. *Alcoutim • Map P1 • (281) 546 004 • alcoutim@movijovem.pt • €*

4 Pousada da Juventude Faro
Handily sited if you want advice on jobs and youth discounts from the Instituto Português da Juventude. Also close to Faro's historic centre and ferries to the Ria Formosa sand dune islands. *Rua da Polícia de Segurança, Pública 1, Edificio do IPJ, Faro • Map K6 • (289) 826 521 • faro@movijovem.pt • No air conditioning • €*

5 Pousada da Juventude Portimão
Situated about 4 km (2 miles) north of town, the hostel – which is spacious and inviting – makes up for its lack of proximity to the beach and sights with a tennis court and pool. There is also an indoor billiards and table tennis area. *Lugar do Coca Maravilhas, Portimão • Map E4 • (282) 491 804 • portimao@movijovem.pt • No air conditioning • €*

6 Pousada da Juventude Vila Real de Santo António
Set in a quiet street off Praça Marquês de Pombal, this is a cosy and homely place to stay. There's a small bar area, where guests can get plenty of information about nearby sights and activities, including river cruises along the Guadiana. *Rua Dr Sousa Martins 40, Vila Real de Santo António • Map P4 • (281) 544 565 • No air conditioning • vrsantonio@movijovem.pt • €*

7 Pousada da Juventude Almograve (Alentejo)
Enjoying an enviable coastal location, this hostel offers internet access on site and some great beaches close by. Apartments are also available. *Rua do Chafariz, Almograve, Odemira • (283) 640 000 • No air conditioning • €*

8 Pousada da Juventude Beja (Alentejo)
A modern facility within 20 minutes' walk of Beja's cultural attractions. Free internet access available, as well as a games room and laundry. *Rua Prof. Janeiro Acabado, 7800 Beja • (284) 325 458 • beja@movijovem.pt • No air conditioning • €*

9 Pousada da Juventude Portalegre (Alentejo)
About 20 minutes on foot from the town centre, the Portalegre hostel is more functional than cosy, but has shops, cafés and restaurants close by. *Estrada do Bonfim, Apartado 2, 7300 Portalegre • (245) 330 971 • portalegre@movijovem.pt • No air conditioning • €*

10 Pousada da Juventude Sines (Alentejo)
Nearby lagoon beaches make the Sines hostel an attractive option, though it does have its own pool set in grounds of trim lawn and dwarf palms. *Rua da Floresta, Edificio E, Sines • (269) 635 361 • sines@movijovem.pt • No air conditioning • €*

Price Categories

For a standard, double room per night (with breakfast if included), taxes and extra charges.

€	under €50
€€	€50–€100
€€€	€100–€200
€€€€	€200–€300
€€€€€	over €300

Left **Villa interior** Right **www.algarve-agency.com**

TOP 10 Self-Catering Agents

1 Travel Algarve
A UK agency that specializes in providing holiday breaks in villas and selected hotels in the Algarve. The number of bedrooms in the villas varies from one to six. Special offers are available from time to time. *16 Stamford Street, Stalybridge, Cheshire, UK • (0161) 304 0707 • www.travelalgarve.com*

2 Algarve Retreats
A holiday company that lists a variety of carefully selected quality villas, apartments and hotels in the western Algarve and the historic town of Lagos. The specialist agency can also arrange car hire on your behalf. *Algarve Retreats Ltd, 8 Gypsum Way, Draycott in the Clay, Ashbourne, Derbyshire, UK • (0870) 742 8100 • www.algarve-retreats.com*

3 Villas and Rentals
Primarily a website (and rather a creative one), with colour photographs accompanying detailed descriptions of various properties. Luxury Algarve villas abound along the coast, while farmhouses predominate in inland locales. *11 Priory Mall, Market Square, St Neots, Huntingdon, Cambridgeshire, UK • (0148) 088 0001 • www.villasandrentals.com*

4 Absolute Algarve
A wide range of villas and apartments on offer, including many based near and around golf courses. The Absolute Algarve website also has useful links to other related sites. *Gothic House, 3 The Green, Richmond, Surrey, UK • (020) 894 0161 • www.absolutealgarve.com*

5 Algarve Agency
Offering one of the largest selections of luxury Algarve villas and self-catering apartments for rent, the UK-based Algarve Agency also lists hotels in major resorts. Golf, flight information and late bargains are also at hand. *293 Darwen Road, Bromly Cross, Bolton, Lancashire, UK • (0870) 750 5450 • www.algarveagency.com*

6 Villa Plus
An extensive catalogue of luxury villas with private swimming pools for rent located in some of the most sought-after areas in the Algarve. The website is well illustrated throughout with colour photographs of the villas. *Drover House, 16 Adelaide Street, St Albans, Hertfordshire, UK • (01727) 836 686 • www.villaplus.co.uk*

7 The Real Algarve
A handpicked portfolio of the finest holiday villas, resort property, town houses and farmhouses for rent or sale. *Tamarind, Brackenhill, Caythorpe, Nottinghamshire, UK • (0115) 966 3661 • www.therealalgarve.com*

8 Global Home Network
US agency with detailed pages on Portugal's Algarve region. The website includes listings of country villas to rent in peaceful hilltop locations and charming coastal properties. *1110-D Eldon Street, Suite 106, Herndon, VA, USA • (700) 318-7081 • www.globalhomenetwork.com*

9 International Rentals
An attractive website listing a number of farmhouses typical of rural Algarve. The directory also includes private guesthouses in the region. *P.O. Box 1434, Boston, MA, USA • (617) 233 6892 • www.internationalrentals.com*

10 Rent Villas
This agency features quality properties to rent in the Algarve resorts of Carvoeiro, Tavira and Albufeira, among other locations. Also has villas in the pretty inland village of Alte. *700 E.Main Street, Ventura, CA, USA • (805) 641 1650 • www.rentvillas.com*

Index

Acknowledgements

The Author
Paul Bernhardt is a freelance travel writer and photographer who lives in Portugal.

Produced by BLUE ISLAND PUBLISHING
Editorial Director Rosalyn Thiro
Art Director Stephen Bere
Associate Editor Michael Ellis
Designer Lee Redmond
Picture Research Ellen Root
Research Assistance Amaia Allende
Main Photographers
Paul Bernhardt, Linda Whitwam
Index Jane Simmonds
Fact Checker Mark Harding

AT DORLING KINDERSLEY
Publisher Douglas Amrine
Managing Editor Anna Streiffert
Senior Art Editors Marisa Renzullo, Ian Midson
Senior Cartographic Editor
Casper Morris
DTP Jason Little
Production Melanie Dowland

Picture Credits
The publishers would like to thank all the museums, archaeological sites, hotels, restaurants, bars, clubs, shops, galleries and other establishments for their assistance and kind permission to photograph:

Placement Key: t=top; tl=top left; tr=top right; tc=top centre; trc=top right centre; c=centre; ca=centre above; cra=centre right above; cb=centre below; cr=centre right; b=bottom; bra=bottom right above; bl=bottom left; br=bottom right; l=left

PAUL BERNHARDT: 58tl, 59t, 66c.

MARY EVANS PICTURE LIBRARY: 34tr, 34b, 35tr.

GETTY IMAGES/HULTON ARCHIVE: Keystone 35tl.

MUSEU ARQUEOLOGICO, ALBUFEIRA: 44tl; MUSEU DA CORTICA DA FABRICA DO INGLES, SILVES: 44tr; MUSEU DR.JOSE FORMOSINHO DE LAGOS: 22tl, 22tr, 22c, 23tl; MUSEU MARITIMO, FARO: Carlos Porfirio 45b.

REGAIAO TURISMO DO ALGARVE: 58tc; ROBERTHARDING.COM: 44bl, 44br, 45t.

TRAVEL LIBRARY: Stuart Black 1, 94-5.

PETER WILSON: 12–13.

Jacket
CORBIS: Tony Arruza main image.

DK PICTURE LIBRARY: Paul Harris F/C tc; Linda Whitwam F/C b; Francesca Yorke B/C tl/tr, F/C cla/clb; B/C tc.

Cartography Credits
James Macdonald, Rob Clynes (Mapping Ideas Ltd)

Phrase Book

In an Emergency

Help!	**Socorro!**	soo-**koh**-roo
Stop!	**Páre!**	**pahr'**
Call a doctor!	**Chame um médico!**	**shahm'** ooñ **meh**-dee-koo
Call an ambulance!	**Chame uma ambulância!**	**shahm'** oo-muh **añ**-boo-**lañ**-see-uh
Call the police!	**Chame a polícia!**	**shahm'** uh poo-**lee**-see-uh
Call the fire brigade!	**Chame os bombeiros!**	**shahm'** oosh bom-**bay**-roosh
Where is the nearest telephone?	**Há um telefone aqui perto?**	**ah** ooñ te-le-**fon'** uh-**kee** **pehr**-too
Where is the nearest hospital?	**Onde é o hospital mais próximo?**	ond' **eh** oo **ohsh**-pee-**tahl' mysh** **pro**-see-moo

Communication Essentials

Yes	**Sim**	**seeñ**
No	**Não**	**nowñ**
Please	**Por favor/ Faz favor**	poor fuh-**vor** **fash** fuh-**vor**
Thank you	**Obrigado/da**	o-bree-**gah**-doo/duh
Excuse me	**Desculpe**	dish-**koolp'**
Hello	**Olá**	oh-**lah**
Goodbye	**Adeus**	a-**deh**-oosh
Good morning	**Bom-dia**	boñ **dee**-uh
Good afternoon	**Boa-tarde**	**boh**-uh **tard'**
Good night	**Boa-noite**	**boh**-uh **noyt'**
Yesterday	**Ontem**	oñ-**tayñ**
Today	**Hoje**	**ohj'**
Tomorrow	**Amanhã**	**ah**-mañ **yañ**
Here	**Aqui**	uh-**kee**
There	**Ali**	uh-**lee**
What?	**O quê?**	**oo** keh
Which?	**Qual?**	**kwahl'**
When?	**Quando?**	**kwañ**-doo
Why?	**Porquê?**	**poor**-keh
Where?	**Onde?**	**oñd'**

Useful Phrases

How are you?	**Como está?**	**koh**-moo **shtah**
Very well, thank you.	**Bem, obrigado/da.**	**bayñ** o-bree **gah**-doo/duh
Pleased to meet you.	**Encantado/da.**	eñ-kañ-**tah**-doo/ duh
See you soon.	**Alté logo.**	uh-**teh loh**-goo
That's fine.	**Está bem.**	**shtah bayñ**
Where is/are...?	**Onde está/ estão...?**	**ond' shtah/ shtowñ**
How far is it to...?	**A que distância fica...?**	uh kee dish-**tañ**-see-uh **fee**-kuh
Which way to...?	**Como se vai para...?**	**koh**-moo seh **vy** puh-ruh
Do you speak English?	**Fala Inglês?**	**fah**-luh eeñ-**glehsh**
I don't understand.	**Não compreendo.**	nowñ kom-pree-**eñ**-doo
I'm sorry.	**Desculpe.**	dish-**koolp'**
Could you speak more slowly please?	**Pode falar mais devagar por favor?**	**pohd'** fuh-**lar** **mysh** d'-va-**gar** poor fah-**vor**

Useful Words

big	**grande**	**grañd'**
small	**pequeno**	pe-**keh**-noo
hot	**quente**	**keñt'**
cold	**frio**	**free**-oo
good	**bom**	**boñ**
bad	**mau**	**mah**-oo
enough	**bastante**	bash-**tañt'**
well	**bem**	**bayñ**
open	**aberto**	a-**behr**-too
closed	**fechado**	fe-**shah**-doo
left	**esquerda**	**shkehr**-duh
right	**direita**	dee-**ray**-tuh
straight on	**em frente**	ayñ **freñt'**
near	**perto**	**pehr**-too
far	**longe**	**loñj'**
up	**suba**	**soo**-bah
down	**desça**	**deh**-shuh
early	**cedo**	**seh**-doo
late	**tarde**	**tard'**
entrance	**entrada**	eñ-**trah**-duh
exit	**saída**	sa-**ee**-duh
toilets	**casa de banho**	**kah**-zuh d' **bañ**-yoo
more	**mais**	**mysh**
less	**menos**	**meh**-noosh

Making a Telephone Call

I'd like to place an international call.	**Queria fazer uma chamada internacional.**	**kree**-uh fuh-**zehr** oo-muh sha-**mah**-duh in-ter-na-**see**-oo-**nahl'**
a local call	**uma chamada local**	**oo**-muh sha-**mah**-duh loo-**kahl'**
Can I leave a message?	**Posso deixar uma mensagem?**	**poh**-soo day-**shar oo**-muh meñ-**sah**-jayñ

Shopping

How much does this cost?	**Quanto custa isto?**	**kwañ**-too **koosh**-tuh **eesh**-too
I would like...	**Queria...**	**kree**-uh
I'm just looking.	**Estou só a ver obrigado/a.**	**shtoh soh** uh **vehr** o-bree-**gah**-doo/uh
Do you take credit cards?	**Aceita cartões de crédito?**	uh-**say**-tuh kar-**toinsh** de **kreh**-dee-too?
What time do you open?	**A que horas abre?**	uh **kee oh**-rash **ah**-bre?
What time do you close?	**A que horas fecha?**	uh **kee oh**-rash **fay**-shuh?
this one	**este**	**ehst'**
that one	**esse**	**ehss'**
expensive	**caro**	**kah**-roo
cheap	**barato**	buh-**rah**-too
size (clothes/ shoes)	**número**	**noom'**-roo
white	**branco**	**brañ**-koo
black	**preto**	**preh**-too
red	**roxo**	**roh**-shoo
yellow	**amarelo**	uh-muh-**reh**-loo
green	**verde**	**vehrd'**
blue	**azul**	uh-**zool'**

Types of Shop

antique shop	**loja de antiguidades**	**loh**-juh de añ-tee-gwee-**dahd'sh**
bakery	**padaria**	**pah**-duh-**ree**-uh
bank	**banco**	**bañ**-koo
bookshop	**livraria**	lee-vruh-**ree**-uh
butcher	**talho**	**tah**-lyoo
cake shop	**pastelaria**	pash-te-luh-**ree**-uh
chemist	**farmácia**	far-**mah**-see-uh
fishmonger	**peixaria**	pay-shuh-**ree**-uh
hair dresser	**cabaleireiro**	kab'-lay-**ray**-roo
market	**mercado**	mehr-**kah**-doo
newsagent	**kiosque**	kee-**yohsk'**
post office	**correios**	koo-**ray**-oosh
shoe shop	**sapataria**	suh-puh-tuh-**ree**-uh
supermarket	**supermercado**	soo-**pehr**-mer-**kah**-doo
tobacconist	**tabacaria**	tuh-buh-kuh-**ree**-uh
travel agency	**agência de viagens**	uh-jen-**see**-uh de vee-**ah**-jayñsh

Sightseeing

cathedral	**sé**	**seh**
church	**igreja**	ee-**gray**-juh
garden	**jardim**	jar-**deeñ**
library	**biblioteca**	bee-blee-oo-**teh**-kuh
museum	**museu**	**moo**-zeh-oo
tourist information	**posto de turismo**	posh-**too** d' too-**reesh**-moo
closed for holidays	**fechado para férias**	fe-**sha**-doo puh-ruh **feh**-ree-ash
bus station	**estação de autocarros**	shta-sowñ d' oh-too-**kah**-roosh
railway station	**estação de comboios**	shta-**sowñ** d' koñ-**boy**-oosh
azulejo	uh-zoo-**lay**-joo	painted ceramic tile
Manuelino	ma-noo-el-**ee**-oo	Manueline (late Gothic architectural style)

Staying in a Hotel

Do you have a vacant room?	**Tem um quarto livre?**	**tayñ** ooñ **kwar**-too **leevr'**
room with a bath	**um quarto com casa de banho**	ooñ **kwar**-too koñ **kah**-zuh d' bañ-**yoo**
shower	**duche**	**doosh**
single room	**quarto individual**	**kwar**-too een-dee-vee-doo-**ahl'**
double room	**quarto de casal**	**kwar**-too d' kuh-**zhal'**
twin room	**quarto com duas camas**	**kwar**-too koñ **doo**-ash **kah**-mash
porter	**porteiro**	poor-**tay**-roo
key	**chave**	**shahv'**
I have a reservation.	**Tenho um quarto reservado.**	**tayñ**-yoo ooñ **kwar**-too re-ser-**vah**-doo

Eating Out

Have you got a table for ...?	**Tem uma mesa para ... ?**	**tayñ** oo-muh **meh**-zuh puh-ruh
I'd like to reserve a table.	**Quero reservar una mesa.**	**keh**-roo re-zehr-**var** oo-muh **meh**-zuh
The bill, please.	**A conta por favor/faz favor.**	uh **kohn**-tuh poor fuh-**vor**/ **fash** fuh-**vor**
I am a vegetarian.	**Sou vegetariano/a.**	Soh ve-je-tuh-ree-**ah**-noo/uh
Waiter!	**Por favor!/ Faz favor!**	poor tuh-**vor** **fash** fuh-**vor**
the menu	**a lista**	uh **leesh**-tuh
fixed-price menu	**a ementa turística**	uh ee-**mehñ**-tuh too-**reesh**-tee-kuh
wine list	**a lista de vinhos**	uh **leesh**-tuh de **veeñ**-yoosh
glass	**um copo**	ooñ **koh**-poo
bottle	**uma garrafa**	oo-muh guh-**rah**-fuh
half bottle	**meia-garrafa**	**may**-uh guh-**rah**-fuh
knife	**uma faca**	oo-mah **fah**-kuh
fork	**um garfo**	ooñ **gar**-foo
spoon	**uma colher**	oo-muh kool-**yair**
plate	**um prato**	ooñ **prah**-too
breakfast	**pequeno-almoço**	pe-**keh**-noo-ahl-**moh**-soo
lunch	**almoço**	ahl-**moh**-soo
dinner	**jantar**	jan-**tar**
cover	**couvert**	koo-**vehr**
starter	**entrada**	eñ-**trah**-duh
main course	**prato principal**	**prah**-too prin-see-**pahl'**
dish of the day	**prato do dia**	**prah**-too doo **dee**-uh
set dish	**combinado**	koñ-bee-**nah**-doo
half portion	**meia-dose**	may-uh **doh**-se
dessert	**sobremesa**	**soh**-bre-**meh**-zuh
rare	**mal passado**	**mahl'** puh-**sah**-doo
medium	**médio**	**meh**-dee-oo
well done	**bem passado**	**bayñ** puh-**sah**-doo

Menu Decoder

abacate	uh-buh-**kaht'**	avocado
açorda	uh-**sor**-duh	bread-based stew (often seafood)
açúcar	uh-soo-**kar**	sugar
água mineral	**ah**-gwuh mee-ne-**rahl'**	mineral water
alho	**ay**-oo	garlic
alperce	ahl'-**pehrce**	apricot
amêijoas	uh-may-**joo**-ash	clams
ananás	uh-nuh-**nahsh**	pineapple
arroz	uh-**rohsh**	rice
assado	uh-**sah**-doo	baked
atum	uh-**tooñ**	tuna
aves	**ah**-vesh	poultry
azeite	uh-**zayt'**	olive oil
azeitonas	uh-zay-**toh**-nash	olives

bacalhau	buh-kuh-**lyow**	dried, salted cod
banana	buh-**nah**-nuh	banana
batatas	buh-**tah**-tash	potatoes
batatas fritas	buh-**tah**-tash **free**-tash	french fries
batido	buh-**tee**-doo	milk-shake
bica	**bee**-kuh	espresso
bife	**beef**	steak
bolacha	boo-**lah**-shuh	biscuit
bolo	**boh**-loo	cake
borrego	boo-**reh**-goo	lamb
caça	**kah**-ssuh	game
café	kuh-**feh**	coffee
camarões	kuh-muh-**roysh**	large prawns
caracóis	kuh-ruh-**koysh**	snails
caranguejo	kuh-rañ **gay**-yoo	crabs
carne	**karn'**	meat
cataplana	kuh-tuh-**plah**-nah	sealed wok used to steam dishes
cebola	se-**boh**-luh	onion
cerveja	sehr-**vay**-juh	beer
chá	**shah**	tea
cherne	**shern'**	stone bass
chocolate	shoh-koh-**laht'**	chocolate
chocos	**shoh**-koosh	cuttlefish
choriço	shoh-**ree**-soo	red, spicy sausage
churrasco	shoo-**rash**-coo	on the spit
cogumelos	koo-goo-**meh**-loosh	mushrooms
cozido	koo-**zee**-doo	boiled
enguias	eñ-**gee**-ash	eels
fiambre	fee-**añbr'**	ham
fígado	**fee**-guh-doo	liver
frango	**frañ**-goo	chicken
frito	**free**-too	fried
fruta	**froo**-tuh	fruit
gambas	**gañ**-bash	prawns
gelado	je-**lah**-doo	ice cream
gelo	jeh-**loo**	ice
goraz	goo-**rash**	bream
grelhado	grel-**yah**-doo	grilled
iscas	**eesh**-kash	marinated liver
lagosta	luh-**gohsh**-tuh	lobster
laranja	luh **rañ**-juh	orange
leite	**layt'**	milk
limão	lee-**mowñ**	lemon
limonada	lee-moo-**nah**-duh	lemonade
linguado	leeñ-**gwah**-doo	sole
lulas	**loo**-lash	squid
maçã	muh-**sañ**	apple
manteiga	mañ-**tay**-guh	butter
mariscos	muh-**reesh**-koosh	seafood
meia-de-leite	**may**-uh-d' **layt'**	white coffee
ostras	**osh**-trash	oysters
ovos	**oh**-voosh	eggs
pão	**powñ**	bread
pastel	pash-**tehl'**	cake
pato	**pah**-too	duck
peixe	**paysh'**	fish
peixe-espada	**paysh'-shpah**-duh	scabbard fish
pimenta	pee-**meñ**-tuh	pepper
polvo	**pohl'**-voo	octopus
porco	**por**-coo	pork
queijo	**kay**-joo	cheese
sal	**sahl'**	salt
salada	suh-**lah**-duh	salad
salsichas	sahl-**see**-shash	sausages
sandes	**sañ**-desh	sandwich
sopa	**soh**-puh	soup
sumo	**soo**-moo	juice
tamboril	tañ-boo-**ril'**	monkfish
tarte	**tart'**	pie/cake
tomate	too-**maht'**	tomato
torrada	too-**rah**-duh	toast
tosta	**tohsh**-tuh	toasted sandwich
vinagre	vee-**nah**-gre	vinegar
vinho branco	**veeñ**-yoo **brañ**-koo	white wine
vinho tinto	**veeñ**-yoo **teeñ**-too	red wine
vitela	vee-**teh**-luh	veal

Numbers

0	**zero**	**zeh**-roo
1	**um**	**ooñ**
2	**dois**	**doysh**
3	**três**	**tresh**
4	**quatro**	**kwa**-troo
5	**cinco**	**seeñ**-koo
6	**seis**	**saysh**
7	**sete**	**set'**
8	**oito**	**oy**-too
9	**nove**	**nov'**
10	**dez**	**desh**
11	**onze**	**oñz'**
12	**doze**	**doz'**
13	**treze**	**trez'**
14	**catorze**	ka-**torz'**
15	**quinze**	**keeñz'**
16	**dezasseis**	de-zuh-**saysh**
17	**dezassete**	de-zuh-**set'**
18	**dezoito**	de-**zoy**-too
19	**dezanove**	de-zuh-**nov'**
20	**vinte**	**veent'**
21	**vinte e um**	**veen-tee**-ooñ
30	**trinta**	**treeñ**-tuh
40	**quarenta**	kwa-**reñ**-tuh
50	**cinquenta**	seen-**kweñ**-tuh
60	**sessenta**	se-**señ**-tuh
70	**setenta**	se-**teñ**-tuh
80	**oitenta**	oy-**teñ**-tuh
90	**noventa**	noo-**veñ**-tuh
100	**cem**	**sayñ**
101	**cento e um**	**señ**-too-ee-ooñ
102	**cento e dois**	**señ**-too-ee-**doysh**
200	**duzentos**	doo-**zeñ**-toosh
300	**trezentos**	tre-**zeñ**-toosh
400	**quatrocentos**	**kwa**-troo-**señ**-toosh
500	**quinhentos**	kee-**nyeñ**-toosh
600	**seiscentos**	saysh-**señ**-toosh
700	**setecentos**	set'-**señ**-toosh
800	**oitocentos**	**oy**-too-**señ**-toosh
900	**novecentos**	nov'-**señ**-toosh
1,000	**mil**	**meel'**

Time

one minute	**um minuto**	ooñ mee-**noo**-too
one hour	**uma hora**	**oo**-muh **oh**-ruh
half an hour	**meia-hora**	**may**-uh **oh**-ruh
Monday	**segunda-feira**	se-**goon**-duh-**fay**-ruh
Tuesday	**terça-feira**	ter-sa-**fay**-ruh
Wednesday	**quarta-feira**	**kwar**-ta-**fay**-ruh
Thursday	**quinta-feira**	**keen**-ta-**fay**-ruh
Friday	**sexta-feira**	**say**-shta-**fay**-ruh
Saturday	**sábado**	**sah**-ba-too
Sunday	**domingo**	doo-**meen**-goo